SPHERE OF
INFLUENCE MASTERY

UNLOCK THE POWER OF PERSONAL CONNECTIONS TO BUILD A THRIVING REAL ESTATE BUSINESS AND SECURE YOUR SUCCESS

BRANDON JOHNSON

ISBN: 979-8-89079-292-1 (paperback)
ISBN: 979-8-89079-293-8 (ebook)

JETLAUNCH

Table of Contents

Introduction

In the dynamic and competitive world of real estate, building and nurturing your sphere of influence is crucial for long-term success. Your sphere of influence includes everyone you know personally and professionally—friends, family, colleagues, clients, and acquaintances. These are the people who can refer you to potential clients, provide testimonials, and support your business in numerous ways. Understanding how to effectively engage and maintain these relationships can set you apart from the competition.

Sphere of Influence Mastery is designed to provide realtors with practical, actionable strategies to strengthen their connections and foster loyalty within their networks. Each chapter delves into different aspects of nurturing your sphere of influence, from leveraging social media and hosting community events to personalized gestures and professional development. By implementing these methods, you can build a solid foundation of trust and rapport with your contacts, ultimately driving more business and ensuring sustainable growth.

Real estate is not just about transactions; it's about relationships. Successful realtors understand the importance of cultivating and maintaining strong connections. This book aims to guide you through this process, offering detailed insights and step-by-step instructions on effectively nurturing your sphere of influence. Whether you're a seasoned professional or just starting in the industry, the strategies outlined here will provide valuable tools to enhance your real estate practice.

In the following chapters, we will explore various techniques to engage with your sphere of influence, providing you with a comprehensive roadmap to becoming a more effective and influential realtor. From traditional methods to innovative digital strategies, you'll find a wealth of information that can be tailored to your unique style and market. Let's embark on this journey together and unlock the potential of your network.

1

Understanding Your Sphere of Influence

Your sphere of influence (SOI) is one of your most valuable assets. It comprises all the people you know—friends, family, past clients, acquaintances, and anyone with whom you have a personal or professional relationship. Understanding how to identify, manage, and nurture your SOI is crucial for building a successful real estate business.

What is a Sphere of Influence?

Your sphere of influence includes individuals who trust and respect you, making them more likely to refer you to others or use your services themselves. These people can be powerful advocates for your business, helping you generate leads and grow your client base.

Your SOI can be categorized into three main groups:

1. **Primary SOI**: This group includes your closest relationships—family members, close friends, and best clients. These people know you well and are most likely to advocate for your services.
2. **Secondary SOI**: These are people you know but are not as close to—acquaintances, colleagues, and friends of friends. They may not know you as intimately, but they still have a favorable impression of you and are willing to recommend your services.
3. **Tertiary SOI**: This group includes people you don't know directly but are connected to you through mutual acquaintances, social networks, or professional affiliations. They might not be aware of your services yet, but they have the potential to become valuable contacts.

The Importance of Nurturing Your SOI

Nurturing your sphere of influence is about building and maintaining relationships. People are more likely to do business with someone they trust, and nurturing your SOI helps establish that trust. By staying in touch, offering value, and showing genuine interest in your contacts, you strengthen your relationships and keep yourself top-of-mind when they or someone they know needs a real estate agent.

There are several key reasons why nurturing your SOI is essential:

1. **Lead Generation**: Your SOI can be a significant source of referrals and repeat business. When you

maintain strong relationships, your contacts are more likely to recommend you to others or use your services again.

2. **Brand Ambassadorship**: People within your SOI can become brand ambassadors, spreading the word about your services and helping you build your reputation within the community.

3. **Market Insight**: Your SOI can provide valuable insights into the market, as they are often part of the community you serve. They can share neighborhood trends, buyer preferences, and other relevant data.

4. **Business Stability**: A well-nurtured SOI provides a stable foundation for your business. A loyal SOI can help sustain your business through referrals and repeat clients, even during market downturns.

Strategies for Identifying and Expanding Your SOI

To effectively nurture your sphere of influence, you must first identify who belongs to it and consider ways to expand it. Here's how you can do that:

1. Identify Your Existing SOI

Start by making a comprehensive list of everyone you know. This includes:

- **Family and Friends**: Immediate and extended family, close friends, and acquaintances
- **Professional Contacts**: Colleagues, past and present clients, mentors, and industry peers

- **Community Members**: Neighbors, members of local organizations or clubs, and people you interact with in your community
- **Social Media Connections**: Friends, followers, and connections on platforms like Facebook, LinkedIn, Instagram, and Twitter

Categorize your list into the three groups mentioned earlier: primary, secondary, and tertiary. This will help you prioritize your efforts based on the strength of your relationship with each group.

2. Expand Your SOI

Expanding your SOI involves actively seeking new connections. Here are some ways to do that:

- **Join Local Groups**: Participate in local clubs, organizations, or community groups related to your interests or the real estate industry. This provides opportunities to meet new people and expand your network.
- **Attend Networking Events**: Regularly attend industry events, conferences, and social gatherings. These events are prime opportunities to meet new contacts and expand your SOI.
- **Leverage Social Media**: Engage with your social media followers by sharing valuable content, commenting on posts, and participating in online discussions. This can help you connect with a broader audience and attract potential clients.

- **Volunteer in the Community**: Volunteering for local causes or events is a great way to meet new people and demonstrate your commitment to the community. It can also lead to meaningful connections that enhance your SOI.

Best Practices for Nurturing Your SOI

Once you've identified and expanded your SOI, the next step is to nurture these relationships. Here are some best practices for doing so:

1. Consistent Communication

Regular communication is key to maintaining relationships. This doesn't mean you need to be constantly in touch, but you should have a consistent presence in your contacts' lives. Consider the following:

- **Personalized Emails**: Send personalized emails to check in with your contacts, share updates, or provide valuable information. Tailor your messages to the interests and needs of everyone.
- **Phone Calls and Texts**: Sometimes, a quick phone call or text can be more effective than an email. Use these methods for more personal or urgent communications.
- **Social Media Engagement**: Stay active on social media by liking, commenting, and sharing posts from your contacts. This helps maintain visibility and shows that you're engaged with what's happening in their lives.

- **Client Appreciation**: Periodically reach out with appreciation messages or small tokens of gratitude to your clients. A personalized thank-you card, a small gift, or a simple message can go a long way in showing you value their business.

2. Provide Value

One of the most effective ways to nurture your SOI is by consistently providing value. When you offer something of value, your contacts are more likely to engage with you and view you as a trusted resource. Here's how you can provide value:

- **Educational Content**: Share valuable insights, tips, and advice on real estate. This could include market updates, home maintenance tips, or investment strategies.
- **Exclusive Opportunities**: Offer your SOI early access to new listings, special events, or exclusive promotions. This makes them feel valued and encourages them to stay connected.
- **Problem Solving**: Be proactive in helping your contacts solve problems or address challenges. Whether it's finding a contractor or providing advice on a real estate issue, your willingness to assist builds trust and loyalty.

3. Personalize Your Interactions

Personalization is key to making your contacts feel valued and appreciated. Personalizing your interactions shows that you've taken the time to consider their unique needs and preferences. Here are some ways to personalize your interactions:

- **Remember Important Dates**: Keep track of important dates, such as birthdays, anniversaries, or significant milestones. Acknowledging these occasions with a call, card, or gift can strengthen your relationships.
- **Tailor Your Messages**: Avoid generic communications. Instead, tailor your messages to reflect your knowledge of the individual's interests, preferences, or recent activities.
- **Follow Up on Past Conversations**: Refer to previous conversations in your communications. For example, if a client mentioned they were planning a home renovation, ask how it's going in your next conversation.

4. Build a Community

Creating a sense of community among your SOI can lead to stronger relationships and a more engaged network. Here's how you can foster a community:

- **Host Events**: Organize events that bring your SOI together, such as client appreciation parties, community picnics, or real estate seminars. These events provide opportunities for networking and relationship-building.
- **Create Online Groups**: Consider creating a private Facebook or LinkedIn group for your SOI. Use this space to share valuable content, facilitate discussions, and connect your contacts with each other.

- **Encourage Networking**: Introduce your contacts to each other when appropriate. For example, if you know two clients who could benefit from each other's services, make an introduction.

Action Item: Creating an SOI Management Plan

To effectively nurture your SOI, it's important to have a structured plan in place. Here's how to create an SOI management plan:

Step 1: Organize Your SOI

Use a CRM tool or a simple spreadsheet to organize your SOI. Categorize your contacts into primary, secondary, and tertiary groups, and note any relevant details, such as interests, recent interactions, or referral potential.

Step 2: Develop a Communication Schedule

Create a schedule for regular communication with your SOI. This could include monthly emails, quarterly phone calls, and periodic social media engagements. Tailor the frequency and method of communication to each group.

Step 3: Set Goals and Track Progress

Set specific goals for your SOI management, such as increasing referrals, improving engagement, or expanding your network. Regularly track your progress and adjust your strategy as needed.

Step 4: Review and Adjust

Periodically review your SOI management plan to ensure it's effective. Consider adding new contacts, adjusting your communication frequency, or trying new methods for engagement.

Executing the Method

Start by organizing your SOI into categories and developing a communication schedule. Set specific goals and use a CRM tool to track your interactions. Regularly review and adjust your plan to ensure you're effectively nurturing your sphere of influence.

Understanding and nurturing your sphere of influence is crucial for building a successful real estate business. By identifying your SOI, expanding it strategically, and consistently providing value, you can build strong relationships that lead to referrals, repeat business, and long-term success. With a structured approach and regular communication, you can maintain a thriving network that supports your real estate career.

Action Steps

Identify Your SOI:

- Make a list of everyone you know across all aspects of your life (family, friends, colleagues, social media, etc.).
- Categorize them into primary, secondary, and tertiary groups.

Expand Your SOI:

- Join local clubs and organizations.
- Attend networking events and engage on social media.
- Volunteer in the community to meet new people.

Nurture Your Relationships:

- Communicate regularly with personalized emails, phone calls, and social media engagement.
- Provide value through educational content, problem-solving, and offering exclusive opportunities.
- Personalize your interactions by remembering important dates and tailoring your messages.

Create a Community:

- Host events to bring your SOI together and foster networking.
- Create online groups to facilitate ongoing engagement and community-building.
- Introduce contacts to each other when appropriate to help strengthen relationships.

SOI Management Plan:

- Use a CRM or spreadsheet to organize and track your SOI.
- Develop a communication schedule for consistent engagement.

- Set specific goals for your SOI, such as increasing referrals or expanding your network.
- Review and adjust your plan periodically to ensure effectiveness.

2

Building and Maintaining Authentic Relationships

A uthenticity is crucial for building trust and fostering lasting relationships in the real estate industry. Genuine connections are the foundation of your sphere of influence, and maintaining these relationships with authenticity can lead to a steady stream of referrals and repeat business. This chapter will delve into the importance of authenticity, strategies for building genuine relationships, and tips for maintaining them over time.

The Importance of Authentic Relationships in Real Estate

Authenticity is about being true to yourself and others. In the context of real estate, it means conducting your business with honesty, transparency, and integrity. When you approach your interactions with authenticity, you create trust, which is essential in a field where clients rely on your expertise to make significant financial decisions.

There are several reasons why authenticity is vital in real estate:

1. **Trust Building**: Trust is the cornerstone of any successful relationship, and authenticity is key to establishing it. Clients who believe you have their best interests at heart are more likely to rely on your advice and refer you to others.

2. **Long-Term Relationships**: Authentic relationships are sustainable because they are based on mutual respect and understanding. Clients who feel genuinely connected to you are more likely to return for future transactions and maintain contact over time.

3. **Reputation Management**: In the age of online reviews and social media, your reputation is more visible than ever. Authenticity helps you build a positive reputation, as clients are more likely to share positive experiences when they feel they've been treated with honesty and respect.

4. **Differentiation**: In a competitive industry like real estate, authenticity can set you apart. While many agents may offer similar services, your genuine approach can make you memorable and preferred among clients.

Strategies for Building Authentic Relationships

Building authentic relationships requires effort and intentionality. Here are some strategies to help you establish genuine connections with your clients and within your sphere of influence:

1. Prioritize Transparency

Transparency is a key component of authenticity. Being open and honest in your communications builds trust and demonstrates your commitment to your client's best interests. Here's how you can prioritize transparency:

- **Be Honest About Expectations**: Set realistic expectations with your clients from the outset. Whether it's about the timeline of a transaction, market conditions, or the potential challenges they may face, being upfront ensures there are no surprises later.
- **Communicate Clearly**: Avoid jargon or overly complex explanations. Instead, communicate in a clear and straightforward manner, making sure your clients understand every step of the process.
- **Share Market Insights**: Keep your clients informed about the latest market trends and how they might impact their decisions. This positions you as an expert and shows you're committed to helping them make informed choices.

2. Show Genuine Interest in Your Clients

Authentic relationships are built on mutual interest and respect. Showing genuine interest in your clients as individuals, rather than just potential commissions, can deepen your connections. Here's how:

- **Ask About Their Goals**: Understand your client's long-term goals and how their real estate needs fit into the bigger picture. Whether they're looking for a starter home or an investment property, knowing their objectives allows you to provide more personalized service.

- **Remember Personal Details**: Take note of important details about your clients' lives, such as their family members' names, hobbies, or upcoming life events. Mentioning these details in future conversations shows you care about them beyond the transaction.

- **Follow Up Personally**: After a transaction is complete, follow up with your clients on a personal level. This could be a simple check-in to see how they're settling into their new home or sending a congratulatory message on a significant milestone.

3. Be Consistent in Your Interactions

Consistency is crucial for building trust. When you are consistent in your actions and communications, your clients know what to expect from you, which reinforces your authenticity. Here's how to maintain consistency:

- **Regular Communication**: Stay in touch with your clients and sphere of influence regularly. This could be through monthly newsletters, periodic phone calls, or social media updates. The key is to be present without being overbearing.

- **Deliver on Promises**: If you make a promise, ensure you follow through. Whether it's a small commitment like sending over a document or a larger one like meeting a deadline, consistency in delivering on promises builds reliability.

- **Maintain Your Values**: Stay true to your values in every interaction. Let your principles guide your decisions, whether dealing with a challenging client or negotiating a tough deal. This consistency will enhance your reputation for authenticity.

4. Be Vulnerable When Appropriate

Vulnerability can strengthen relationships by fostering deeper connections. While it's important to maintain professionalism, sharing personal experiences or admitting when you don't have all the answers can make you more relatable and trustworthy. Here's how to appropriately incorporate vulnerability:

- **Share Your Journey**: Occasionally share your real estate experiences, including successes and challenges. This can help clients relate to you and see you as more than just a service provider.
- **Admit Mistakes**: If you make a mistake, own it and take steps to rectify the situation. Clients appreciate honesty and are more likely to forgive errors when you're transparent about them.
- **Be Open to Feedback**: Invite your clients to provide feedback on your services and be open to constructive criticism. This shows you value their opinion and are committed to continuous improvement.

Tips for Maintaining Authentic Relationships Over Time

Building authentic relationships is just the beginning; maintaining them requires ongoing effort. Here are some tips to help you keep your relationships strong and genuine over time:

1. Stay Connected Beyond Transactions

One of the most common mistakes real estate agents make is losing touch with clients after completing a transaction. To maintain authentic relationships, it's important to stay connected even when there's no immediate business need:

- **Check-In Regularly**: Periodically reach out to your past clients just to check-in. This could be a phone call, an email, or even a holiday card. The goal is to remind them that you value the relationship, not just the transaction.

- **Offer Ongoing Support**: Let your clients know you're available for any real estate-related questions or needs they might have, even after the sale is complete. Whether they need a recommendation for a contractor or advice on market trends, being a continued resource helps keep the relationship alive.

- **Celebrate Milestones**: Acknowledge important milestones in your clients' lives, such as anniversaries of their home purchase, birthdays, or other significant events. Sending a card, a small gift, or even just a congratulatory message can go a long way in maintaining the relationship.

2. Personalize Your Communications

Personalization is key to maintaining authenticity. Generic messages can feel insincere and may weaken your connection with clients. Here's how to keep your communications personalized:

- **Tailor Your Messages**: When sending emails or making phone calls, personalize your messages based on your previous interactions with the client. Reference specific conversations, past transactions, or personal details that show you remember and value them.
- **Segment Your Contacts**: Use your CRM to segment your contacts based on their interests, past transactions, or relationships with you. This allows you to send more relevant and personalized content, whether it's a market update, holiday greeting, or home maintenance tip.
- **Be Responsive**: Promptly respond to your clients' communications and try to address their inquiries or concerns in a way that reflects your knowledge of their unique situation. This responsiveness demonstrates that you prioritize their needs.

3. Provide Continued Value

To keep your relationships strong, it's important to continue providing value even when there's no immediate transaction. Here are some ways to do that:

- **Share Market Insights**: Keep your clients informed about market trends, neighborhood developments, and other relevant information. Regularly sharing valuable insights keeps you top-of-mind and reinforces your role as a trusted advisor.

- **Offer Exclusive Resources**: Provide your clients with access to exclusive resources, such as early notifications about new listings, invitations to real estate seminars, or special discounts with local businesses. This shows that you're continuously looking out for their interests.

- **Educate and Empower**: Offer educational content that empowers your clients to make informed decisions. This could include guides on buying or selling a home, tips for home improvement, or advice on real estate investment.

4. Be Genuine in Your Appreciation

Showing genuine appreciation for your clients is essential for maintaining authentic relationships. When clients feel appreciated, they are more likely to remain loyal and refer you to others. Here's how to express appreciation authentically:

- **Say Thank You**: A simple thank-you message can go a long way in showing your clients that you value their business. Whether it's a handwritten note, a phone call, or a small gift, expressing gratitude makes your clients feel appreciated.

- **Celebrate Their Successes**: When your clients achieve a goal, such as buying their first home or selling a property quickly, celebrate their success with them. Acknowledge their achievement and share in their excitement.

- **Give Back**: Consider giving back to your clients and community to show your appreciation. This could be through charitable donations in their name, organizing community events, or offering discounts to repeat clients.

Action Item: Developing an Authentic Relationship Plan

It's helpful to develop a structured plan to ensure you're consistently building and maintaining authentic relationships. Here's how to create one:

Step 1: Assess Your Current Relationships

Start by assessing your current relationships. Identify which relationships are strong and which may need more attention. Consider factors such as the frequency of communication, the level of trust, and the history of interactions.

Step 2: Set Relationship Goals

Set specific goals for each relationship. For example, you might aim to deepen your connection with a particular client by meeting them for coffee or strengthen a weak relationship by increasing your communication frequency.

Step 3: Create a Communication Plan

Develop a communication plan that outlines how and when you'll reach out to each contact. This plan should include personalized messages, regular check-ins, and opportunities to provide value.

Step 4: Track and Adjust

Regularly track your progress and adjust your plan as needed. If a particular strategy isn't working, don't be afraid to try something new. The key is to remain consistent and genuine in your efforts.

Executing the Method

Begin by assessing your current relationships and identifying areas for improvement. Set specific goals and create a communication plan that includes personalized interactions and regular check-ins. Track your progress and adjust your plan to ensure you're maintaining authentic and meaningful relationships with your sphere of influence.

Building and maintaining authentic relationships is essential for long-term success in the real estate industry. By prioritizing transparency, showing genuine interest in your clients, and consistently providing value, you can create lasting connections that lead to repeat business and referrals. Remember that authenticity is not just a strategy; it's a way of conducting business that reflects your commitment to integrity and your client's best interests. With a structured approach and a focus on genuine interactions, you can cultivate a thriving network of authentic relationships that will support your real estate career for years to come.

Action Steps

Prioritize Transparency:

- Set realistic expectations with clients from the start.
- Communicate clearly and avoid jargon to ensure understanding.
- Share market insights to position yourself as a trusted advisor.

Show Genuine Interest in Clients:

- Ask about clients' long-term goals and how real estate fits into their plans.
- Remember personal details to make clients feel valued.
- Follow up personally after transactions to strengthen connections.

Be Consistent:

- Stay in touch with regular communication (e.g., monthly newsletters, phone calls).
- Always deliver on promises, no matter how small.
- Maintain your core values in every interaction, reinforcing your authenticity.

Incorporate Vulnerability (When Appropriate):

- Share personal experiences, including both successes and challenges.
- Admit mistakes openly and work to resolve them.

- Encourage client feedback to demonstrate openness and a commitment to improvement.

Maintain Authentic Relationships Over Time:

- Check-in with clients periodically and offer ongoing support.
- Celebrate milestones and show appreciation with personalized messages or gifts.
- Offer continued value through market insights, exclusive resources, and educational content.

Develop an Authentic Relationship Plan:

- Assess your current relationships to identify strengths and areas for improvement.
- Set specific relationship goals for each client, aiming to deepen connections.
- Create a communication plan that outlines when and how you'll reach out.
- Regularly track your progress and adjust your plan as necessary.

3

Leveraging Technology to Enhance Relationships

I n today's digital age, technology plays an increasingly crucial role in the real estate industry. From customer relationship management (CRM) systems to social media, numerous tools can help real estate professionals nurture their sphere of influence more effectively. This chapter will explore how to leverage technology to enhance your relationships, streamline your processes, and maintain a strong connection with your clients.

The Role of Technology in Real Estate Relationships

Technology offers several benefits for real estate professionals looking to build and maintain strong relationships:

1. **Efficiency**: Technology allows you to automate routine tasks, freeing up time to focus on building genuine connections with your clients.
2. **Scalability**: With the right tools, you can manage many contacts and ensure no one falls through the cracks, regardless of how large your sphere of influence becomes.
3. **Personalization**: Technology enables you to gather and organize data about your clients, allowing for more personalized and relevant interactions.
4. **Consistency**: Automated reminders and scheduled communications help ensure you stay in regular contact with your clients, maintaining consistency in your relationships.

Tools and Strategies for Leveraging Technology

To effectively leverage technology in nurturing your sphere of influence, consider the following tools and strategies:

1. Implement a Customer Relationship Management (CRM) System

A CRM system is essential for any real estate professional looking to manage their contacts efficiently. It allows you to store detailed client information, track interactions, and set follow-up reminders. Here's how to get the most out of your CRM:

- **Centralize Client Information**: Use your CRM to keep all relevant client information in one place. This includes contact details, transaction history, notes from past conversations, and any specific preferences or needs they've expressed.

- **Segment Your Contacts**: Organize your contacts into different segments based on criteria such as location, type of client (buyer, seller, investor), or where they are in the sales funnel. This segmentation allows you to tailor your communications and marketing efforts more effectively.

- **Automate Follow-Ups**: Set up automated reminders for follow-ups after specific milestones, such as a year after a home purchase or six months after a property sale. This ensures you stay in touch with clients at key times without needing to remember every detail manually.

- **Track Interactions**: Use your CRM to log all client interactions, including emails, phone calls, and meetings. This record helps you maintain continuity in your communications and ensures you're always current on your client's needs and concerns.

2. Utilize Social Media for Relationship Building

Social media platforms are powerful tools for maintaining a presence in your clients' lives and nurturing your sphere of influence. Here's how to effectively use social media for relationship building:

- **Engage Consistently**: Regularly post updates about the real estate market, share useful tips, and engage with your followers by responding to comments and messages. Consistent activity keeps you top-of-mind for your audience.

- **Showcase Your Personality**: Use social media to show the human side of your business. Share behind-the-scenes glimpses of your work, personal anecdotes, or community involvement. This helps clients connect with you on a more personal level.

- **Use Targeted Ads**: Social media platforms offer sophisticated targeting options for ads. Use these to reach specific segments of your sphere of influence, such as past clients or prospects in a particular geographic area. Targeted ads can help reinforce your presence and keep your services front and center.

- **Host Live Events**: Consider hosting live events on platforms like Facebook or Instagram, where you can interact with your audience in real-time. These events include Q&A sessions, virtual home tours, or market updates. Live events create an interactive experience that strengthens your connection with your followers.

3. Leverage Email Marketing for Personalized Communication

Email marketing remains one of the most effective ways to nurture relationships in real estate. Here's how to leverage email marketing to stay connected with your sphere of influence:

- **Segment Your Email List**: Like with your CRM, segment your email list based on client type, interests, and location. This allows you to send more targeted and relevant content to different groups of clients.

- **Personalize Your Emails**: Use the data you've collected in your CRM to personalize your email communications. Address clients by name, reference past transactions, and tailor the content to their specific interests or needs.

- **Send Regular Newsletters**: Create a monthly or quarterly newsletter that provides valuable content to your clients, such as market updates, tips for buying or selling, and community news. Regular newsletters help you stay top-of-mind and position you as an expert in your field.

- **Automate Drip Campaigns**: Set up automated email campaigns that send a series of emails over time based on specific triggers, such as a client expressing interest in a particular type of property. Drip campaigns keep your clients engaged and informed without requiring constant manual effort.

4. Use Video Content to Engage and Educate

Video content is increasingly popular and can be a powerful tool for building relationships in real estate. Here's how to incorporate video into your relationship-building strategy:

- **Create Market Update Videos**: Share regular market update videos that provide insights into current trends, pricing, and opportunities in your local market. Video allows you to communicate complex information in an engaging and easily digestible format.

- **Produce Property Tours**: Offer virtual tours of properties through video. This showcases your listings and provides value to clients who may be unable to visit in person. Property tours also demonstrate your dedication to providing comprehensive service.

- **Share Educational Content**: Create videos that educate your clients on various aspects of real estate, such as the home-buying process, financing options, or tips for preparing a home for sale. Educational content positions you as an expert and provides lasting value to your clients.

- **Host Webinars**: Consider hosting webinars on topics relevant to your clients, such as investment opportunities, market forecasts, or first-time homebuyer tips. Webinars offer a way to interact with a large audience while providing valuable information.

5. Incorporate AI and Automation for Enhanced Efficiency

Artificial intelligence (AI) and automation tools can further enhance your efficiency and effectiveness in nurturing relationships. Here's how to incorporate these technologies into your strategy:

- **Chatbots for Immediate Responses**: Use AI-powered chatbots on your website or social media platforms to provide immediate responses to common inquiries. Chatbots can handle basic questions, schedule appointments, and direct clients to relevant resources, ensuring no inquiry goes unanswered.

- **Automated Lead Scoring**: Use AI to automatically score and prioritize leads based on their likelihood to convert. This lets you focus your efforts on the most promising prospects, increasing efficiency and effectiveness.

- **Predictive Analytics**: Leverage predictive analytics to identify trends and opportunities within your sphere of influence. For example, AI can analyze data to predict which clients are most likely to be interested in selling their home or investing in a new property, allowing you to reach out proactively.

- **Personalized Marketing**: AI can analyze data from various sources to create highly personalized marketing campaigns that resonate with individual clients. This level of personalization can significantly improve engagement and conversion rates.

Balancing Technology and Personal Touch

While technology offers many benefits, balancing it with a personal touch is essential. Here are some tips for maintaining this balance:

1. Personalize Automated Communications

While automation can save time, ensuring automated communications don't feel impersonal is important. Personalize your automated emails and messages as much as possible by including the client's name, referencing past interactions, and tailoring the content to their interests or needs.

2. Use Technology to Enhance–Not Replace–Human Interaction

Technology should complement—not replace—your personal interactions with clients. Use tools like CRM systems and social media to stay organized and informed, but follow up with phone calls, in-person meetings, or handwritten notes that add a personal touch.

3. Be Available for Personal Contact

Ensure your clients know they can reach you directly when needed. While chatbots and automated responses are useful, nothing replaces the value of a personal conversation when a client has a specific concern or question.

4. Monitor and Adjust Your Approach

Regularly assess how your use of technology is impacting your relationships. If you find that clients are feeling disconnected or that communications are becoming too impersonal, adjust your approach to reintroduce more personal interactions.

Action Item: Integrating Technology into Your Relationship-Building Strategy

To effectively integrate technology into your relationship-building strategy, follow these steps:

Step 1: Assess Your Current Technology Use

Start by evaluating the tools and technologies you're currently using. Identify any gaps in your tech stack or areas where you could use technology more effectively to enhance your relationships.

Step 2: Choose the Right Tools

Based on your assessment, select the tools that best fit your needs. Choose technologies that align with your goals and workflow, whether it's a CRM system, social media platform, or email marketing service.

Step 3: Develop a Technology Integration Plan

Create a plan for integrating the selected tools into your daily operations. This plan should include how you'll use each tool to enhance your relationships and any necessary training or setup processes.

Step 4: Monitor and Refine

Regularly monitor the impact of your technology use on your relationships and refine your approach as needed. This could involve tweaking your CRM settings, adjusting your social media strategy, or experimenting with new forms of content.

Executing the Method

Begin by assessing your current use of technology and identifying areas for improvement. Choose the right tools that align with your goals and develop a plan for integrating them into your workflow. Monitor the impact on your relationships and adjust as needed to ensure technology is enhancing rather than detracting from your personal connections.

Leveraging technology is essential for modern real estate professionals looking to nurture their sphere of influence. Using tools like CRM systems, social media, and AI, you can enhance efficiency, personalize your interactions, and maintain strong relationships with your clients. However, balancing technology with a personal touch is crucial to ensure your connections remain genuine and meaningful. With the right approach, technology can be a powerful ally in building and sustaining a thriving network of relationships in the real estate industry.

Action Steps

Implement a CRM System:

- Centralize all client information in one place, including contact details and transaction history.
- Segment contacts by location, type (buyer, seller, investor), or position in the sales funnel for targeted communications.
- Automate follow-ups and track interactions to ensure consistent and timely communication.

Utilize Social Media:

- Engage consistently by sharing relevant content and responding to comments and messages.
- Showcase your personality by sharing behind-the-scenes glimpses of your business and personal life.
- Use targeted ads and host live events (e.g., Q&As, virtual tours) to interact directly with your audience.

Leverage Email Marketing:

- Segment your email list and send personalized messages tailored to client interests and needs.
- Create regular newsletters with valuable content like market updates, tips for buying or selling, and local news.
- Automate drip campaigns to keep clients engaged without constant manual effort.

Incorporate Video Content:

- Create regular market update videos to share insights and engage with clients.
- Produce virtual property tours for prospective buyers unable to visit in person.
- Share educational videos on home-buying, financing, or preparing a home for sale.
- Host webinars to provide in-depth advice and engage with larger audiences.

Use AI and Automation:

- Implement AI-powered chatbots to respond quickly to common inquiries on your website or social media.
- Use automated lead scoring to prioritize promising leads based on their likelihood to convert.
- Leverage predictive analytics to identify trends and proactively reach out to clients likely to be interested in buying or selling.

Balance Technology with Personal Touch:

- Personalize automated communications by including client names and referencing past interactions.
- Use technology to enhance communication but always follow up with personal touchpoints like phone calls, meetings, or handwritten notes.
- Be accessible for direct, personal contact when necessary to address specific concerns.

Integrate Technology into Your Strategy:

- Assess your current technology tools and identify areas for improvement.
- Select the tools that best align with your goals and workflow.
- Develop a plan for integrating these tools into your daily operations and train your team if needed.
- Monitor the impact of these tools on your relationships and adjust your approach as necessary.

4

Hosting Memorable Events to Strengthen Connections

I n the real estate industry, face-to-face interactions remain among the most powerful ways to build and nurture relationships. Hosting memorable events is an excellent strategy for connecting with your sphere of influence on a personal level. These events allow you to showcase your expertise, express your appreciation, and create lasting memories that keep you top-of-mind with your clients. In this chapter, we'll explore the different types of events you can host, how to plan and execute them effectively, and how to ensure they resonate with your audience.

The Power of Events in Real Estate

Events create a unique platform for building deeper connections with your clients and prospects. They allow you to:

1. **Personalize Your Brand**: Events give you the opportunity to showcase your personality and the human side of your business, helping clients feel more connected to you.

2. **Provide Value**: Whether through educational seminars or community gatherings, events allow you to offer value to your clients, reinforcing your role as a trusted advisor.

3. **Create Shared Experiences**: Shared experiences, such as attending an event together, can create lasting memories and a sense of community, which strengthens the bond between you and your clients.

4. **Generate Referrals**: A well-executed event can lead to word-of-mouth referrals as attendees share their positive experiences with friends and family.

Types of Events to Host

When planning events to nurture your sphere of influence, consider the following types of gatherings:

1. Client Appreciation Events

Client appreciation events are a great way to show gratitude to your existing clients while keeping you at the forefront of their minds. These events can range from simple gatherings to more elaborate celebrations. Examples include:

- **Holiday Parties**: Host a festive holiday party where clients can mingle, enjoy refreshments, and celebrate the season with you. This type of event shows appreciation and provides a natural opportunity to reconnect with clients before the new year.

- **Picnics or BBQs**: A casual outdoor event like a picnic or BBQ is perfect for families and allows clients to relax and enjoy a fun day out. It's also a great way to engage with clients in a more informal setting.

- **Thank-You Dinners**: Invite a select group of top clients to an intimate dinner as a special thank-you for their continued support. This type of event fosters deeper connections with your most valuable clients.

2. Educational Seminars and Workshops

Educational events provide value by positioning you as a knowledgeable resource in the real estate industry. Consider hosting:

- **Homebuying Seminars**: Educate first-time homebuyers on the process, from securing financing to finding the right property. These seminars can attract both existing clients and new prospects.

- **Investment Workshops**: Offer workshops on real estate investing, covering topics like market trends, property management, and financing options. This type of event appeals to clients interested in growing their real estate portfolios.

- **Home Maintenance Clinics**: Partner with local contractors or home improvement stores to offer clinics on home maintenance, such as winterizing a home or preparing a property for sale. This practical advice is valuable to homeowners and positions you as a go-to resource.

3. Community Events

Community events allow you to connect with clients while contributing to the local community. These events can help establish you as a community leader and build goodwill. Examples include:

- **Charity Fundraisers**: Organize a fundraiser to support a local cause or non-profit organization. Not only does this event allow you to give back, but it also provides a platform for clients to participate in a meaningful way.
- **Neighborhood Block Parties**: Host a block party in a neighborhood where you have sold multiple homes. This event fosters a sense of community among residents and positions you as an integral part of the neighborhood.
- **Local Festivals or Markets**: Sponsor or host a booth at a local festival or market, where you can engage with the community, offer information about the real estate market, and showcase your properties.

4. Exclusive Property Tours

Exclusive property tours offer a unique opportunity to showcase high-end listings while providing an exclusive experience for select clients. Consider:

- **VIP Open Houses**: Host VIP open houses for luxury listings, inviting high-net-worth clients to an exclusive preview. Offer refreshments, live music, or other amenities to create a luxurious atmosphere.

- **Neighborhood Tours**: Organize a tour of a specific neighborhood or development, highlighting properties for sale and the community's amenities. This type of event is particularly effective for clients interested in a specific area.
- **New Development Previews**: If you can access new developments before they hit the market, invite clients for a sneak peek. This exclusive access can create a sense of urgency and excitement.

Planning and Executing a Successful Event

Hosting a successful event requires careful planning and attention to detail. Here's how to ensure your event is a success:

1. Define Your Objectives

Before planning your event, clearly define your objectives. Are you aiming to show appreciation, generate leads, or educate your audience? Understanding your goals will help guide your event planning and ensure it aligns with your broader business strategy.

2. Choose the Right Venue

The venue plays a significant role in the success of your event. Consider the following factors when selecting a venue:

- **Accessibility**: Ensure the venue is easily accessible for your clients, with adequate parking and public transportation options.

- **Size**: Choose a venue that comfortably accommodates your guest list without feeling overcrowded or empty.
- **Ambiance**: The venue's ambiance should align with the tone of your event. For example, a luxury property tour should be held in a sophisticated setting, while a casual BBQ might be hosted in a park or backyard.

3. Create a Detailed Agenda

A detailed agenda helps keep your event organized and ensures everything runs smoothly. Your agenda should include:

- **Timeline**: Outline the timeline for the event, including setup, guest arrival, main activities, and teardown.
- **Activities**: Plan the key activities for the event, such as speeches, demonstrations, or entertainment. Ensure these activities align with your event's objectives.
- **Roles and Responsibilities**: Assign specific roles and responsibilities to your team members or volunteers, such as greeting guests, managing registration, or coordinating with vendors.

4. Promote Your Event

Effective promotion is key to ensuring a good turnout for your event. Use a mix of marketing channels to reach your audience, such as:

- **Email Invitations**: Send personalized email invitations to your client list, including all the event details and a clear call-to-action to RSVP.
- **Social Media**: Promote the event on your social media channels, creating buzz and encouraging followers to attend. Consider using event hashtags to increase visibility.
- **Direct Mail**: Send a physical invitation via direct mail for high-value clients or exclusive events. This adds a personal touch and can make the invitation feel more special.
- **Community Partnerships**: Partner with local businesses or organizations to co-host or promote the event, expanding your reach and attracting a broader audience.

5. Provide Exceptional Service

On the day of the event, focus on providing exceptional service to your guests. This includes:

- **Warm Welcome**: Greet each guest personally as they arrive, making them feel valued and appreciated.
- **Attentive Hospitality**: Ensure all guests are comfortable and have everything they need, whether it's refreshments, seating, or information.
- **Engaging Activities**: Keep guests engaged with interesting activities, presentations, or entertainment that align with the event's theme and objectives.

6. Follow Up After the Event

The follow-up is just as important as the event itself. Here's how to follow up effectively:

- **Thank-You Notes**: Send personalized thank-you notes or emails to all attendees, expressing your appreciation for their participation and reinforcing your connection.
- **Share Event Highlights**: Post photos, videos, or highlights from the event on your social media channels or in a follow-up email to attendees. This not only extends the life of the event but also provides content for your marketing efforts.
- **Schedule Follow-Up Meetings**: Use the event as a springboard to schedule follow-up meetings with clients or prospects who attended. This is an opportunity to discuss their needs in more detail and explore potential business opportunities.

Action Item: Planning Your Next Client Event

To plan and execute a successful client event, follow these steps:

Step 1: Identify Your Objective

Determine the primary goal of your event, whether it's client appreciation, education, community engagement, or showcasing properties.

Step 2: Choose a Theme and Venue

Select a theme that aligns with your objective and choose a suitable venue that enhances the event's ambiance and accessibility.

Step 3: Develop a Promotion Plan

Create a comprehensive promotion plan that includes email invitations, social media marketing, and partnerships with local businesses to ensure a strong turnout.

Step 4: Execute with Precision

On the day of the event, focus on delivering exceptional service, engaging activities, and a warm, welcoming atmosphere.

Step 5: Follow Up

After the event, send thank-you notes, share event highlights, and schedule follow-up meetings to capitalize on the momentum.

Executing the Method

Begin by defining the objectives for your event and selecting a theme that resonates with your target audience. Plan the logistics carefully, ensuring the venue, agenda, and promotional efforts align with your goals. Provide exceptional service during the event and follow up promptly to reinforce the connections made. This approach will help you create memorable experiences that strengthen your relationships and keep your clients engaged.

Hosting memorable events is a powerful way to nurture your sphere of influence in the real estate industry. By carefully planning and executing events that provide value, create shared experiences, and showcase your expertise, you can deepen your connections with clients and generate new business opportunities. Whether it's a client appreciation party, an educational seminar, or a community event, creating an experience that resonates with your audience and reinforces your role as a trusted real estate professional is key.

Action Steps

Define Your Objectives:

- Determine the primary goal of your event, such as client appreciation, education, community engagement, or property showcasing.
- Align the event's purpose with your broader business strategy.

Choose the Right Type of Event:

- **Client Appreciation:** Host holiday parties, BBQs, or intimate dinners to show gratitude to your clients.
- **Educational Seminars:** Organize home buying, investing, or home maintenance seminars to provide value and position yourself as an expert.
- **Community Engagement:** Plan charity fundraisers, neighborhood block parties, or sponsor local festivals to establish yourself as a community leader.

- **Exclusive Property Tours:** Arrange VIP open houses or neighborhood tours to offer exclusive access to high-end properties.

Select a Venue:

- Ensure the venue is accessible, appropriately sized, and fits the event's ambiance. Consider factors such as parking, comfort, and alignment with the event's tone (e.g., casual vs. luxury).

Create a Detailed Agenda:

- Plan the event timeline, including guest arrival, main activities, and wrap-up.
- Assign roles to your team members to ensure smooth operations.

Promote the Event:

- Send personalized email invitations and promote the event through social media and direct mail.
- Partner with local businesses to co-host or promote the event, expanding your reach.

Provide Exceptional Service:

- Greet guests warmly, ensure their comfort and keep them engaged with relevant activities or entertainment.
- Maintain a welcoming and professional atmosphere throughout the event.

Follow Up After the Event:

- Send thank-you notes or emails to attendees, reinforcing your connection.
- Share event highlights through photos or videos on social media.
- Schedule follow-up meetings with key prospects or clients who attended the event to discuss their needs in more detail.

Planning Your Next Client Event:

- **Step 1:** Identify your event objective.
- **Step 2:** Choose a theme and suitable venue.
- **Step 3:** Develop a promotion plan, including email, social media, and community partnerships.
- **Step 4:** Execute the event with precision, focusing on exceptional service and engagement.
- **Step 5:** Follow up with attendees to capitalize on the connections made.

5

Building a Strong Online Presence

In today's digital age, having a robust online presence is essential for real estate professionals looking to nurture and expand their sphere of influence. Your online presence is often the first impression potential clients have of you, and it serves as a vital tool for maintaining connections with your existing clients. This chapter will delve into the importance of building a strong online presence, explore the key platforms and strategies to utilize and provide actionable steps to enhance your digital footprint.

The Importance of an Online Presence

A strong online presence offers numerous benefits for real estate professionals:

1. **Increased Visibility**: A well-crafted online presence makes it easier for potential clients to find you when

searching for real estate services. This visibility can lead to more inquiries and opportunities.

2. **Brand Authority**: Consistent, high-quality online content helps establish you as an authority in your field. When clients see that you regularly share valuable insights and information, they are more likely to trust you with their real estate needs.

3. **Client Engagement**: Social media and other online platforms provide direct communication with your audience, allowing you to engage with clients and prospects regularly.

4. **Lead Generation**: A strong online presence can generate leads by driving traffic to your website or capturing contact information through landing pages and forms.

5. **Reputation Management**: Online platforms give you control over your brand's narrative. By actively managing your online reputation, you can address negative feedback, highlight positive reviews, and showcase your successes.

Key Components of a Strong Online Presence

To build and maintain a strong online presence, focus on the following key components:

1. Professional Website

Your website is the cornerstone of your online presence. It serves as your digital storefront, where clients can learn more about your services, browse listings, and contact you directly.

Here's what to consider when building or updating your website:

- **User-Friendly Design**: Ensure your website is easy to navigate, with a clean and modern design. Users should be able to find information quickly without digging through cluttered pages.

- **Mobile Responsiveness**: A significant portion of web traffic comes from mobile devices. Make sure your website is optimized for mobile viewing, with responsive design elements that adapt to different screen sizes.

- **Search Engine Optimization (SEO)**: Implement SEO best practices to ensure your website ranks well in search engine results. This includes using relevant keywords, optimizing page load speed, and creating high-quality content.

- **Compelling Content**: Your website should feature a blog or resource section where you regularly post articles, market updates, and other valuable content. This helps with SEO and positions you as an industry expert.

- **Lead Capture Tools**: Incorporate lead capture tools such as contact forms, chatbots, and calls-to-action (CTAs) to encourage visitors to contact you or sign up for your newsletter.

2. Social Media Presence

Social media platforms are critical for connecting with your audience, sharing content, and building your brand. Here's how to effectively use social media to nurture your sphere of influence:

- **Platform Selection**: Focus on the most relevant platforms to your audience. For real estate professionals, Facebook, Instagram, LinkedIn, and YouTube are typically the most effective.
- **Consistent Branding**: Ensure your branding is consistent across all social media platforms, including your profile pictures, cover images, and bios. This consistency helps reinforce your brand identity.
- **Engaging Content**: Post a mix of content that includes property listings, market insights, client testimonials, and personal updates. Use a variety of formats, such as photos, videos, stories, and live streams, to keep your audience engaged.
- **Regular Posting Schedule**: Consistency is key to maintaining a strong social media presence. Develop a posting schedule that ensures you regularly share content and interact with your audience.
- **Audience Engagement**: Engage with your followers by responding to comments, answering questions, and participating in discussions. Social media is a two-way street, so active engagement is crucial.

3. Online Reviews and Testimonials

Positive online reviews and testimonials can significantly impact your reputation and influence potential clients. Here's how to leverage them:

- **Encourage Reviews**: After successfully closing a transaction, kindly ask your clients to leave a review on platforms like Google, Zillow, or Facebook. Provide them with direct links to make the process easy.

- **Showcase Testimonials**: Display testimonials prominently on your website and social media profiles. Highlight specific successes and client experiences to build credibility.
- **Respond to Reviews**: Always respond to reviews, both positive and negative. Thank clients for their feedback, and address any concerns raised in negative reviews professionally and constructively.
- **Case Studies**: Create detailed case studies that showcase your work with specific clients, highlighting the challenges faced, solutions provided, and the outcomes achieved. These can be powerful tools for demonstrating your expertise.

4. Email Marketing

Email marketing is a highly effective way to stay in touch with your sphere of influence and nurture leads over time. Here's how to optimize your email marketing efforts:

- **Build Your List**: Continuously grow your email list by offering valuable content or incentives, such as a free market report, in exchange for contact information.
- **Segment Your Audience**: Segment your email list based on factors such as client type (buyers, sellers, investors), location, or stage in the buying process. This allows you to send targeted, relevant content to each group.
- **Personalize Your Emails**: Use personalization techniques, such as addressing recipients by name and tailoring content to their specific interests or needs.

- **Valuable Content**: Provide valuable content in your emails, such as market updates, new listings, tips for homebuyers or sellers, and community news. Avoid overly promotional content, focusing instead on building relationships.

- **Consistent Sending Schedule**: Develop a consistent email schedule, whether it's a weekly newsletter or monthly market update. Consistency helps keep your audience engaged and looking forward to your communications.

5. Online Advertising

Online advertising can amplify your reach and help you target specific audiences. Consider the following advertising strategies:

- **Google Ads**: Use Google Ads to target potential clients who are actively searching for real estate services. You can create ads that appear in search results or display ads on relevant websites.

- **Social Media Ads**: Platforms like Facebook and Instagram offer robust advertising tools that allow you to target specific demographics, interests, and behaviors. Use these tools to promote your listings, events, or content.

- **Retargeting Ads**: Retargeting ads are a powerful way to stay in front of people who have already visited your website or engaged with your content. These ads can help keep your brand top-of-mind as potential clients move closer to making a decision.

Action Item: Enhancing Your Online Presence

To build a strong online presence, follow these steps:

Step 1: Audit Your Current Online Presence

Begin by auditing your current online presence. Review your website, social media profiles, and online reviews to identify areas for improvement. Consider how well your branding, content, and engagement efforts align with your goals.

Step 2: Develop a Content Strategy

Create a content strategy that includes regular blog posts, social media updates, and email campaigns. Focus on providing value to your audience, showcasing your expertise, and maintaining consistency across all platforms.

Step 3: Optimize for Search Engines

Implement SEO best practices on your website and content. Research relevant keywords, optimize your site's structure, and ensure your content is valuable and informative.

Step 4: Engage with Your Audience

Make a concerted effort to engage with your audience across all online platforms. Respond to comments, answer questions, and participate in discussions to build relationships and foster loyalty.

Step 5: Invest in Online Advertising

Consider investing in online advertising to boost your visibility and reach targeted audiences. Experiment with different ad formats and platforms to see what works best for your business.

Executing the Method

Start by thoroughly auditing your existing online presence and identifying strengths and areas for improvement. Develop a comprehensive content strategy that focuses on value and consistency. Optimize your online assets for search engines, ensuring potential clients can easily find you. Engage regularly with your audience across social media and other online platforms, and consider online advertising to extend your reach. By following these steps, you'll build a strong online presence that enhances your credibility, attracts new clients, and keeps you connected with your sphere of influence.

In the modern real estate industry, a strong online presence is not just a luxury; it's a necessity. Your online presence serves as the foundation for building and maintaining relationships with your clients and prospects. Investing in a professional website, engaging on social media, leveraging online reviews, and implementing effective email marketing and advertising strategies can create a powerful digital footprint supporting your long-term success. Consistency and authenticity are key to nurturing your sphere of influence online and ensuring your brand stands out in a competitive market.

Action Steps

Audit Your Current Online Presence:

- Review your website, social media profiles, and online reviews to identify areas for improvement.
- Evaluate how your branding, content, and engagement align with your goals and target audience.

Develop a Content Strategy:

- Create a strategy for regular blog posts, social media updates, and email campaigns that provide value to your audience.
- Ensure consistency across platforms, positioning yourself as an expert and resource.

Optimize Your Website for SEO:

- Research and implement relevant keywords to improve your website's ranking in search engines.
- Ensure your website is user-friendly, mobile-responsive, and optimized for search engine visibility.

Engage with Your Audience:

- Respond to comments, questions, and messages across social media platforms and your website.
- Actively participate in discussions to build relationships and strengthen client loyalty.

Invest in Online Advertising:

- Experiment with Google Ads and social media ads to reach targeted audiences.
- Use retargeting ads to stay in front of potential clients who have already interacted with your content.

Leverage Social Media Platforms:

- Focus on platforms like Facebook, Instagram, LinkedIn, and YouTube that are most relevant to your audience.
- Post a mix of content (e.g., property listings, market insights, client testimonials) to keep followers engaged.

Request and Showcase Reviews:

- Encourage satisfied clients to leave reviews on platforms like Google and Zillow.
- Display positive testimonials prominently on your website and social media to build credibility.

6

Leveraging Community Involvement to Build Relationships

B uilding a successful real estate career isn't just about closing deals and managing transactions; it's also about establishing strong, lasting relationships within your community. Being actively involved in your community not only enhances your personal and professional reputation but also creates opportunities to connect with potential clients and strengthen your existing relationships. This chapter will explore how community involvement can help you nurture your sphere of influence, the types of activities you can engage in, and practical steps to integrate community involvement into your real estate strategy.

The Impact of Community Involvement

Community involvement is a powerful tool for real estate professionals for several reasons:

1. **Building Trust**: Active participation in community events and causes shows you care about the well-being of your community. This builds trust with current and potential clients, who are more likely to do business with someone they see as invested in the same community they live in.
2. **Enhancing Visibility**: Regular involvement in community activities increases your visibility. As people see you consistently contributing to local causes and events, they begin to recognize you as a leader in the community and someone they can rely on for their real estate needs.
3. **Networking Opportunities**: Community events provide natural opportunities to meet new people and expand your network. These connections can lead to referrals and new clients as people get to know you personally.
4. **Personal Fulfillment**: Beyond the professional benefits, community involvement offers a sense of personal fulfillment. Contributing to causes you care about can be rewarding and enrich your life outside of work.

Types of Community Involvement

There are many ways to get involved in your community, each offering different opportunities to connect with others and strengthen your influence. Consider the following options:

1. Volunteering

Volunteering your time and skills is a direct way to contribute to your community. Consider the following types of volunteer activities:

- **Local Charities and Non-Profits**: Partner with local charities or non-profits that align with your values. Whether it's helping to organize events, participating in fundraising activities, or offering your professional services, your involvement will be appreciated and recognized.
- **Youth and Education Programs**: Get involved with local schools or youth programs. This could involve sponsoring school events, coaching sports teams, or participating in career days. Supporting the next generation is a meaningful way to give back and connect with families in your community.
- **Community Clean-Ups**: Join or organize community clean-up events. These activities improve the neighborhood's appearance and foster a sense of community pride and ownership.

2. Sponsorships

Sponsoring local events or teams is another effective way to get involved and increase your visibility. Consider the following sponsorship opportunities:

- **Sports Teams**: Sponsor a local sports team, such as a Little League baseball team or a community soccer league. Your logo on team uniforms and banners at games can increase your brand recognition.

- **Community Events**: Sponsor local festivals, fairs, or charity events. In exchange for your sponsorship, you may receive advertising space, mentions in event promotions, or the opportunity to set up a booth to interact with attendees.

- **School Programs**: Many schools seek sponsorships for events like fundraisers, field trips, or extracurricular activities. Sponsoring these programs can strengthen your connection with families and educators in your community.

3. Organizing Events

Taking the initiative to organize community events can significantly boost your profile and provide valuable networking opportunities. Consider the following types of events:

- **Real Estate Seminars**: Host educational seminars on topics such as home buying, selling, or investing. These events provide value to your community while showcasing your expertise.

- **Charity Drives**: Organize charity drives or fundraising events for causes that resonate with your community. Whether it's a food drive, coat collection, or benefit concert, these events show your commitment to helping those in need.

- **Networking Mixers**: Host networking events for local business owners, residents, and professionals. These mixers can help you build relationships with other community leaders and potential clients.

4. Joining Local Organizations

Becoming an active member of local organizations can deepen your community ties and provide ongoing opportunities to connect with others. Consider joining:

- **Chamber of Commerce**: Your local Chamber of Commerce is a hub for business activity in the community. Joining allows you to network with other business owners, participate in events, and stay informed about local economic trends.
- **Neighborhood Associations**: Participate in or join the board of your neighborhood association. This involvement keeps you informed about community issues and gives you a voice in local decisions that could affect property values and development.
- **Civic and Service Clubs**: Organizations like Rotary, Kiwanis, or Lions Club offer opportunities to engage in service projects and community improvement initiatives. Membership in these clubs can enhance your reputation as a community-minded professional.

Integrating Community Involvement into Your Real Estate Strategy

Community involvement should be an integral part of your overall real estate strategy. Here's how to effectively integrate it:

1. Align with Your Values

Choose community involvement activities that align with your personal and professional values. Whether it's supporting education, improving local infrastructure, or helping the less fortunate, aligning with causes you genuinely care about will make your involvement more meaningful and authentic.

2. Set Clear Objectives

Define what you want to achieve through your community involvement. Your objectives could include increasing your visibility, building trust, generating leads, or simply giving back. Having clear goals will help you choose the right activities and measure their impact.

3. Leverage Your Skills and Resources

Use your skills and resources as a real estate professional to contribute to your community. For example, offer free real estate workshops, provide market analysis reports to neighborhood associations, or use your negotiation skills to help local non-profits secure better deals on property.

4. Balance Time and Effort

While community involvement is important, balancing it with your other professional responsibilities is crucial. Choose activities that fit your schedule and allow you to contribute meaningfully without overextending yourself.

5. Promote Your Involvement

Don't be shy about sharing your community involvement. Use your online platforms, such as your website, social media, and email newsletters, to highlight the events you're involved in, the causes you support, and the impact of your contributions. This promotes the causes you care about and reinforces your commitment to the community.

6. Build Relationships Through Participation

Community involvement is about building relationships, not just visibility. Take the time to connect with other participants, engage in meaningful conversations, and follow up after events to solidify the connections you've made.

Action Item: Enhancing Your Community Involvement

To increase your community involvement, follow these steps:

Step 1: Identify Causes That Matter to You

Start by identifying causes or organizations that resonate with your values. This will make your involvement more meaningful and sustainable.

Step 2: Research Opportunities

Research opportunities to get involved in your community. Look for local charities, events, and organizations that align with your interests and professional goals.

Step 3: Commit to Regular Participation

Commit to regularly participating in or supporting community activities. Whether volunteering, sponsoring events, or joining organizations, consistent involvement is key to building strong relationships.

Step 4: Leverage Your Platform

Use your online and offline platforms to promote the causes you support and the activities you participate in. Share your experiences and invite others to join you in making a difference.

Executing the Method

Start by identifying community causes that align with your values and professional objectives. Research opportunities to get involved, such as volunteering, sponsoring events, or joining local organizations. Commit to regular participation, ensuring you balance your time and effort. Leverage your platform to promote your involvement and build relationships through meaningful participation. This approach will help you strengthen your community ties and enhance your influence within your sphere.

Community involvement is a powerful way to nurture your sphere of influence and establish yourself as a trusted real estate professional. By actively participating in local events, supporting meaningful causes, and building relationships through community engagement, you can increase your visibility, build trust, and create opportunities for business growth. Remember, authenticity is the key to successful community involvement; choose activities that align with your values and commit to making a genuine difference in your community. With the right approach, your involvement will benefit your business and enrich your personal and professional life.

Action Steps

Identify Causes That Matter to You:

- Choose causes or organizations that resonate with your personal and professional values.
- Focus on activities that align with your long-term goals and contribute to your community.

Research Opportunities for Involvement:

- Look for local charities, events, and organizations that align with your interests.
- Seek opportunities that provide personal fulfillment and professional growth.

Commit to Regular Participation:

- Commit to participate regularly in volunteering, sponsoring events, or joining local organizations.
- Balance community involvement with your professional responsibilities to avoid overextension.

Leverage Your Platform:

- Use your website, social media, and email newsletters to share your community involvement.
- Promote the causes and events you support to reinforce your role as a community-minded real estate professional.

Build Relationships Through Participation:

- Take time to connect with other participants at events and build meaningful relationships.
- Follow up after events to solidify the connections made and foster long-term relationships.

Set Clear Objectives:

- Define what you want to achieve through community involvement, such as increasing visibility, building trust, or generating leads.
- Align your activities with these objectives for greater impact.

Promote Your Involvement:

- Highlight your community involvement on your digital and physical platforms to demonstrate your commitment.
- Share stories and experiences to inspire others to join you in supporting local causes.

7

Mastering Client Communication for Lasting Relationships

Effective client communication is the cornerstone of a successful real estate career. It's not just about conveying information; it's about building and maintaining strong, lasting relationships with your clients. In this chapter, we will explore the principles of effective client communication, strategies for enhancing your communication skills, and practical tips for fostering positive and enduring client relationships.

The Importance of Client Communication

Strong client communication offers several benefits:

1. **Trust Building**: Clear and consistent communication helps build trust with your clients. Clients who

feel informed and heard are more likely to trust your expertise and recommendations.

2. **Enhanced Client Satisfaction**: Effective communication ensures clients' needs and expectations are met. It reduces misunderstandings and helps clients feel valued and appreciated.

3. **Increased Referrals**: Satisfied clients are more likely to refer you to their friends and family. Good communication can lead to positive word-of-mouth and generate new business opportunities.

4. **Problem Resolution**: Effective communication is crucial for addressing and resolving issues that may arise during transactions. Being proactive and transparent helps manage problems before they escalate.

5. **Ongoing Relationships**: Strong communication lays the foundation for long-term relationships with clients. By staying in touch and maintaining regular contact, you keep yourself top-of-mind for future needs and referrals.

Principles of Effective Client Communication

To master client communication, adhere to the following principles:

1. Clarity

Clear communication is essential to avoid misunderstandings. Ensure your messages are straightforward and free of jargon. Use simple language to explain complex concepts and provide clear instructions or information.

2. Consistency

Consistency in communication helps build reliability. Maintain regular contact with your clients through updates, follow-ups, or check-ins. Consistent messaging reinforces your commitment to their needs and helps establish a sense of reliability.

3. Active Listening

Active listening involves fully concentrating on what the client is saying and responding thoughtfully. It means not just hearing their words but understanding their underlying needs and concerns. Reflect on what you've heard to confirm understanding and show empathy.

4. Empathy

Show empathy by acknowledging and validating your clients' feelings and experiences. Empathetic communication helps build rapport and demonstrates that you understand their perspective. This can be especially important during stressful situations like buying or selling a home.

5. Responsiveness

Be prompt in your responses to client inquiries and concerns. Timely communication shows you value their time and are dedicated to addressing their needs. Even if you don't have an immediate solution, acknowledge their message and provide an estimated timeframe for a more detailed response.

6. Personalization

Tailor your communication to each client's preferences and needs. Use their name, reference previous conversations, and customize your approach based on their unique situation. Personalized communication makes clients feel valued and respected.

Strategies for Enhancing Client Communication

To enhance your communication skills and build stronger relationships with your clients, consider implementing the following strategies:

1. Utilize Multiple Channels

Different clients prefer different communication channels. Some prefer phone calls, while others prefer emails or text messages. Offer multiple ways for clients to reach you and be flexible in adapting to their preferred method of communication.

- **Phone Calls**: Great for urgent matters, complex discussions, or building rapport.
- **Emails**: Ideal for detailed information, formal communication, and documentation.
- **Text Messages**: Useful for quick updates and informal communication.
- **Video Calls**: Effective for face-to-face interactions when meeting in person isn't possible.

2. Regular Updates

Keep clients informed throughout the buying or selling process with regular updates. Provide status reports, share market insights, and notify them of any changes or developments. Regular communication helps clients feel engaged and reassured.

- **Weekly Updates**: Summarize progress, market trends, and next steps.
- **Milestone Updates**: Notify clients when significant milestones are reached, such as accepted offers or closing dates.
- **Market Insights**: Share relevant market information to keep clients informed about trends and opportunities.

3. Create a Communication Plan

Develop a communication plan for each client to outline how and when you will stay in touch. This plan can be tailored to their preferences and the specific needs of the transaction.

- **Initial Consultation**: Discuss preferred communication methods and frequency.
- **Transaction Phases**: Outline key points of communication during each phase of the transaction.
- **Post-Transaction Follow-Up**: Plan follow-up communication after completing the transaction to ensure continued satisfaction.

4. Use Technology

Leverage technology to streamline communication and enhance client experience. Consider the following tools:

- **Customer Relationship Management (CRM) Systems**: Manage client information, track interactions, and set follow-up reminders.
- **Automated Email Campaigns**: Send personalized, automated messages for updates, anniversaries, and special occasions.
- **Chatbots**: Respond instantly to common inquiries and capture leads on your website.

5. Provide Value-Added Content

Share valuable content with your clients to enhance their experience and build trust. This content can include:

- **Market Reports**: Provide insights into local real estate trends and market conditions.
- **Home Maintenance Tips**: Share advice on maintaining and improving their property.
- **Community Information**: Offer information about local events, services, and amenities.

6. Seek Feedback

Regularly seek feedback from your clients to gauge their satisfaction and identify areas for improvement. Use surveys, follow-up calls, or informal conversations to gather insights and make necessary adjustments.

- **Post-Transaction Surveys**: Ask clients to rate their experience and provide comments.
- **Follow-Up Calls**: Check in with clients after the transaction to address any lingering concerns and gather feedback.
- **Informal Conversations**: Engage in casual conversations to understand clients' perspectives and preferences.

Practical Tips for Fostering Positive Client Relationships

To nurture lasting relationships with your clients, implement the following practical tips:

1. Be Approachable and Friendly

Adopt a friendly and approachable demeanor in all interactions. Clients are more likely to feel comfortable sharing their needs and concerns if they perceive you as approachable and personable.

- **Warm Greeting**: Start conversations with a friendly greeting and positive attitude.
- **Open Body Language**: Use open body language and maintain eye contact to convey warmth and sincerity.

2. Be Transparent

Transparency builds trust and prevents misunderstandings. Be honest about the process, potential challenges, and any limitations. Clients appreciate transparency and are more likely to trust your guidance.

- **Clear Explanations**: Provide clear explanations for your recommendations and decisions.
- **Address Concerns**: Address any concerns or issues openly and honestly.

3. Celebrate Milestones

Acknowledge and celebrate significant milestones in your clients' real estate journey. Whether it's closing on a new home or completing a successful sale, celebrating these moments reinforces your commitment and shows appreciation.

- **Personalized Gifts**: Consider sending personalized gifts or cards to mark important milestones.
- **Client Appreciation Events**: Host events or gatherings to celebrate successes and show gratitude.

4. Maintain Long-Term Contact

Keep in touch with your clients even after the transaction is complete. Regular follow-ups, newsletters, and event invitations help maintain the relationship and keep you top-of-mind for future needs.

- **Annual Check-Ins**: Schedule annual check-ins to catch up and offer assistance.
- **Newsletters**: Send regular newsletters with market updates, tips, and community news.

- **Special Occasions**: Acknowledge birthdays, anniversaries, and other special occasions with personalized messages or gifts.

Action Item: Enhancing Client Communication

To enhance your client communication, follow these steps:

Step 1: Assess Current Communication Practices

Evaluate your current communication practices to identify strengths and areas for improvement. Consider feedback from clients and analyze how effectively you're meeting their needs.

Step 2: Develop a Communication Plan

Create a detailed communication plan for interacting with clients throughout the transaction process. Include preferred methods, frequency, and key points of contact.

Step 3: Implement Technology Tools

Leverage technology tools to streamline communication and enhance client experience. Explore CRM systems, automated email campaigns, and chatbots to improve efficiency.

Step 4: Seek and Act on Feedback

Regularly seek client feedback to understand their satisfaction levels and make necessary adjustments. Use surveys, follow-up calls, and informal conversations to gather insights.

Executing the Method

Begin by assessing your current communication practices and developing a comprehensive communication plan for each client. Implement technology tools to streamline your processes and enhance efficiency. Regularly seek and act on client feedback to improve your communication strategies. Adopting these practices will build stronger, more positive relationships with your clients, leading to increased satisfaction, referrals, and long-term success in your real estate career.

Mastering client communication is essential for building and nurturing lasting relationships in the real estate industry. By adhering to the principles of clarity, consistency, active listening, empathy, responsiveness, and personalization, you can enhance your communication skills and foster positive relationships with your clients. Implement strategies such as utilizing multiple communication channels, creating a communication plan, leveraging technology, and providing value-added content. Regularly seek feedback and maintain long-term contact to ensure ongoing client satisfaction. Effective client communication will build trust, enhance client relationships, and achieve greater success in your real estate career.

Action Steps

Assess Current Communication Practices:

- Evaluate how well your current communication methods meet client needs and identify areas for improvement.

- Gather client feedback to understand their preferences and satisfaction levels.

Develop a Communication Plan:

- Create a detailed plan for each client, including preferred methods (phone, email, text) and frequency of contact.
- Outline key communication points for each phase of the transaction process.

Implement Technology Tools:

- Use CRM systems to manage client information and track interactions.
- Consider automated email campaigns and chatbots for quick responses and follow-ups.

Seek and Act on Feedback:

- Regularly ask clients for feedback through surveys, follow-up calls, or informal conversations.
- Use this feedback to adjust and improve your communication strategies.

Use Multiple Communication Channels:

- Adapt to clients' preferred communication methods—whether phone calls, emails, text messages, or video calls.
- Offer various ways for clients to reach you to ensure their convenience.

Provide Value-Added Content:

- Share market reports, home maintenance tips, and community news to keep clients informed and engaged.
- Position yourself as a valuable resource in your clients' real estate journey.

Celebrate Milestones:

- Acknowledge significant moments, such as closing a deal or anniversaries, with personalized gifts or messages.
- Host client appreciation events to deepen relationships and show gratitude.

Maintain Long-Term Contact:

- Keep in touch with clients after the transaction with annual check-ins, newsletters, or personal messages.
- Acknowledge special occasions like birthdays or home anniversaries to stay connected.

8

Building a Strong Referral Network

I n real estate, referrals are one of the most effective ways to generate new business. A strong referral network helps you attract new clients and reinforces your reputation as a trusted professional. This chapter will explore the importance of building a referral network, strategies to cultivate and maintain referral sources, and practical steps to leverage referrals for sustained business growth.

The Importance of a Referral Network

A referral network is crucial for several reasons:

1. **Credibility and Trust**: Referrals come with a built-in level of trust. When someone refers a client to you,

they are essentially vouching for your services, which can significantly increase the likelihood of securing new business.

2. **Cost-Effective Marketing**: Referrals are a cost-effective form of marketing. They require less investment than traditional advertising and often lead to higher conversion rates because the prospective client is already predisposed to trust you.

3. **Higher Quality Leads**: Referrals often result in higher quality leads. Referrals typically come from people who have firsthand experience with your services or know your reputation, leading to clients who are more serious and aligned with your expertise.

4. **Stronger Client Relationships**: Building a referral network helps strengthen relationships with existing clients and contacts. When clients refer you to others, it signifies their satisfaction with your services and reinforces their loyalty.

Strategies for Cultivating and Maintaining Referral Sources

To build and maintain a strong referral network, consider implementing the following strategies:

1. Provide Exceptional Service

The foundation of a successful referral network is exceptional service. Satisfied clients are more likely to refer you to others if they have had a positive experience.

- **Exceed Expectations**: Go above and beyond to exceed your client's expectations. Provide personalized attention, address their concerns promptly, and ensure a smooth transaction process.
- **Follow-Up**: After closing a deal, follow up with clients to ensure they are satisfied and address any additional needs or questions. A well-handled post-transaction experience can leave a lasting impression.

2. Build Relationships with Other Professionals

Develop relationships with professionals who can refer clients to you, such as:

- **Mortgage Brokers**: Partner with mortgage brokers who can refer clients seeking real estate services.
- **Home Inspectors**: Build connections with home inspectors who can recommend you to their clients.
- **Contractors and Home Improvement Specialists**: Network with contractors and home improvement specialists who can refer clients looking to buy or sell a home.

3. Leverage Your Sphere of Influence

Your sphere of influence includes friends, family, and acquaintances who can provide referrals. To leverage this network:

- **Stay in Touch**: Regularly communicate with your sphere of influence through newsletters, social media, and personal updates.

- **Ask for Referrals**: Don't hesitate to ask satisfied clients and contacts for referrals. Let them know you appreciate their support and would be grateful for any introductions they can make.

4. Create a Referral Program

Implement a structured referral program to incentivize referrals and track their effectiveness. Consider the following elements:

- **Referral Incentives**: Offer rewards or incentives to clients and partners who refer new business to you. This could include gift cards, discounts on future services, or a charitable donation in their name.
- **Tracking System**: Use a tracking system to monitor referrals and ensure you acknowledge and reward those who refer clients to you.
- **Clear Communication**: Clearly communicate the details of your referral program to clients and partners, including how they can participate and what rewards are available.

5. Network Actively

Engage in networking activities to build relationships and generate referrals. Consider the following approaches:

- **Attend Industry Events**: Participate in real estate industry events, conferences, and trade shows to meet potential referral sources and establish connections.
- **Join Professional Associations**: Become a member of professional associations related to real estate,

such as local real estate boards or industry groups, to expand your network.

- **Engage in Community Activities**: Get involved in community events and organizations to build relationships with local business owners and residents who can refer clients to you.

6. Show Appreciation

Express gratitude to those who refer clients to you. Showing appreciation reinforces positive relationships and encourages continued support.

- **Thank-You Notes**: Send personalized thank-you notes to clients and partners who provide referrals.
- **Recognition**: Publicly recognize and acknowledge those who refer clients to you, such as in newsletters or on social media.
- **Gifts**: Consider sending small tokens of appreciation, such as gift cards or personalized gifts, to show your gratitude.

Practical Steps for Leveraging Referrals

To effectively leverage referrals for business growth, follow these practical steps:

1. Develop a Referral Strategy

Create a referral strategy that outlines how you will generate and manage referrals. This strategy should include:

- **Target Referral Sources**: Identify who you want to build relationships with, such as industry professionals or satisfied clients.
- **Referral Channels**: Determine the channels through which you will solicit referrals, such as email, social media, or in-person meetings.
- **Tracking and Follow-Up**: Establish a system for tracking referrals and following up with those who have been referred to you.

2. Implement Referral Best Practices

Adopt best practices for managing referrals to ensure you make the most of each opportunity:

- **Respond Promptly**: Contact referred clients as soon as possible to demonstrate your enthusiasm and professionalism.
- **Provide Outstanding Service**: Ensure the referred clients receive the same high level of service that earned you the referral in the first place.
- **Keep Referrers Informed**: Update the individuals who referred clients to you about the outcome of the referral. This shows you value their support and keeps them engaged in the process.

3. Evaluate and Adjust Your Approach

Regularly evaluate the effectiveness of your referral network and adjust as needed:

- **Analyze Results**: Review the results of your referral efforts to determine what's working and what's not. Look at metrics such as the number of referrals, conversion rates, and overall satisfaction.
- **Seek Feedback**: Gather feedback from clients and referral sources to understand their experiences and identify areas for improvement.
- **Refine Strategies**: Based on your evaluation, refine your referral strategies and tactics to improve effectiveness and achieve better results.

Action Item: Building and Leveraging Your Referral Network

To build and leverage your referral network, follow these steps:

Step 1: Identify Key Referral Sources

Identify the individuals and professionals who can refer clients to you. This includes current and past clients, industry professionals, and your sphere of influence.

Step 2: Develop a Referral Program

Create a structured referral program with clear incentives and tracking mechanisms. Communicate the program details to your referral sources and encourage participation.

Step 3: Network and Build Relationships

Actively network with potential referral sources through industry events, community activities, and professional associations. Build and nurture relationships with those who can refer clients to you.

Step 4: Show Appreciation and Follow Up

Express gratitude to those who provide referrals and keep them informed about the outcomes. Provide exceptional service to referred clients to reinforce positive relationships.

Executing the Method

Identify key referral sources and develop a referral program with clear incentives and tracking systems. Actively network with potential referral sources and engage in community activities to build relationships. Show appreciation to those who provide referrals and follow up promptly with referred clients. Regularly evaluate and refine your referral strategies to improve effectiveness and achieve better results. Implementing these steps will build a strong referral network that drives business growth and enhances your success in the real estate industry.

Building a strong referral network is essential for achieving long-term success in real estate. You can generate valuable referrals and grow your business by providing exceptional service, cultivating relationships with other professionals, leveraging your sphere of influence, and implementing a structured referral program. Actively network, show appreciation and regularly evaluate your referral strategies to ensure continued success. With a robust referral network, you will enhance your reputation, attract high-quality leads, and achieve sustained growth in your real estate career.

Action Steps

Identify Key Referral Sources:

- Recognize individuals and professionals who can refer clients to you, including past clients, mortgage brokers, home inspectors, contractors, and your sphere of influence.

Provide Exceptional Service:

- Exceed client expectations, follow up after transactions, and ensure a smooth process to increase the likelihood of referrals.

Develop a Referral Program:

- Create a structured program with incentives for referring clients, such as gift cards or donations in their name.
- Use a tracking system to monitor and reward referrals.

Network and Build Relationships:

- Attend industry events, join professional associations, and get involved in community activities to establish connections with potential referral sources.

Leverage Your Sphere of Influence:

- Regularly communicate with your sphere through newsletters, social media, and personal updates.

- Ask satisfied clients and contacts for referrals and express your appreciation for their support.

Show Appreciation:

- Send thank-you notes, publicly recognize referrers, and consider sending small gifts to those who refer clients to you.

Implement Referral Best Practices:

- Respond promptly to referrals, provide outstanding service, and keep referrers informed about the outcome of the referral process.

Evaluate and Refine Your Referral Strategy:

- Regularly review the effectiveness of your referral efforts, analyze metrics, gather feedback, and adjust strategies to improve outcomes.

Follow Up with Referred Clients:

- Provide the same high-quality service to referred clients, ensuring they have a positive experience that reinforces your reputation.

9

Leveraging Social Media for Real Estate Success

S ocial media has transformed how real estate professionals connect with clients, showcase properties, and build
their brands. With the right strategies, social media can
be a powerful tool for nurturing your sphere of influence and
driving business growth. In this chapter, we will explore how
to effectively leverage social media in the real estate industry,
including platform selection, content creation, engagement
tactics, and measurement of success.

The Power of Social Media in Real Estate

Social media offers numerous benefits for real estate professionals:

1. **Increased Visibility**: Social media platforms allow you to reach a broad audience and increase your visibility in the real estate market. You can attract potential clients and build brand awareness by sharing content and engaging with followers.

2. **Enhanced Engagement**: Social media allows for direct interaction with your audience. You can respond to inquiries, engage in conversations, and address client concerns in real-time, fostering stronger relationships and building trust.

3. **Showcasing Properties**: Social media provides an effective platform for showcasing properties through photos, videos, and virtual tours. High-quality content can capture prospective buyers' attention and highlight your listings' unique features.

4. **Building Authority**: Sharing valuable content, such as market insights, tips, and industry news, helps position you as an authority in the real estate field. This can enhance your credibility and attract clients who value your expertise.

5. **Cost-Effective Marketing**: Social media offers a cost-effective way to market your services and properties. With targeted advertising options, you can reach specific demographics and geographic areas without the high costs associated with traditional advertising.

Selecting the Right Social Media Platforms

Different social media platforms offer varying features and audiences. Selecting the right platforms for your real estate business is crucial for maximizing your reach and effectiveness. Consider the following platforms:

1. Facebook

Facebook is one of the most widely used social media platforms, making it a valuable tool for real estate professionals. Key features include:

- **Business Pages**: Create a professional business page to showcase your services, listings, and client testimonials.
- **Groups**: Join or create local real estate groups to connect with potential clients and industry peers.
- **Advertising**: Utilize Facebook ads to target specific demographics and geographic locations with customized ads.

2. Instagram

Instagram is a visually driven platform ideal for showcasing property photos, videos, and virtual tours. Key features include:

- **Visual Content**: Share high-quality images and videos of properties to attract potential buyers.
- **Stories and Reels**: Use Instagram Stories and Reels to share behind-the-scenes content, market updates, and quick tips.
- **Hashtags**: Use relevant hashtags to increase the visibility of your posts and reach a broader audience.

3. LinkedIn

LinkedIn is a professional networking platform suitable for building relationships with industry peers and showcasing expertise. Key features include:

- **Professional Profile**: Maintain a detailed, up-to-date profile highlighting your experience and skills.
- **Content Sharing**: Share articles, market insights, and industry news to position yourself as a thought leader in real estate.
- **Networking**: Connect with other professionals, join industry groups, and participate in discussions.

4. Twitter

Twitter allows for real-time updates and engagement. Key features include:

- **Short-Form Content**: Share concise updates, market trends, and quick tips.
- **Engagement**: Interact with followers and participate in relevant conversations using hashtags and mentions.
- **Trending Topics**: Stay informed about trending topics and join relevant discussions to increase your visibility.

5. YouTube

YouTube is a powerful platform for video content, including property tours, market analyses, and educational videos. Key features include:

- **Property Tours**: Create virtual tours and video walk-throughs of properties to attract potential buyers.
- **Educational Content**: Share videos with tips, market insights, and advice for buyers and sellers.
- **Channel Branding**: Develop a branded YouTube channel to organize and showcase your video content.

Creating Engaging Social Media Content

Content is at the heart of a successful social media strategy. To engage your audience and drive results, focus on creating valuable and compelling content:

1. Property Listings

Showcase your properties with high-quality photos and videos. Highlight key features, unique selling points, and neighborhood amenities.

- **Photo Galleries**: Post visually appealing photo galleries of properties.
- **Video Tours**: Create engaging video tours that provide a comprehensive view of the property.
- **Virtual Open Houses**: Host live virtual open houses to interact with potential buyers in real-time.

2. Market Insights

Share valuable insights about the real estate market, including trends, forecasts, and local market conditions.

- **Infographics**: Create visually appealing infographics to convey market data and trends.
- **Market Reports**: Post regular market reports with updates on housing prices, inventory levels, and economic factors.
- **Expert Analysis**: Offer your analysis and predictions based on current market conditions.

3. Client Testimonials

Showcase positive feedback and testimonials from satisfied clients to build credibility and trust.

- **Text Testimonials**: Share written testimonials from clients.
- **Video Testimonials**: Post video testimonials to capture clients' experiences and emotions.
- **Case Studies**: Highlight successful transactions and the value you provided to clients.

4. Educational Content

Provide valuable information and tips to educate your audience and address common questions.

- **Buying and Selling Tips**: Share tips and advice for buyers and sellers, such as staging tips, financing options, and negotiation strategies.
- **Home Maintenance**: Offer advice on home maintenance and improvement.

- **FAQs**: Address frequently asked questions about the real estate process.

5. Community Involvement

Show your involvement in the community and support for local events and causes.

- **Local Events**: Post about community events, charity drives, and local news.
- **Spotlight Local Businesses**: Highlight local businesses and partners to build connections and support the community.
- **Community Insights**: Share information about neighborhood amenities, schools, and recreational activities.

Engaging with Your Audience

Engagement is key to building relationships and growing your social media presence. Implement the following tactics to enhance engagement:

1. Respond to Comments and Messages

Engage with your audience by promptly responding to comments, messages, and inquiries. Show appreciation for positive feedback and address any concerns or questions.

- **Timely Responses**: Aim to respond to comments and messages within twenty-four hours.

- **Personalized Replies**: Use personalized replies to show you value each interaction.
- **Encourage Interaction**: Ask questions and encourage followers to share their thoughts and experiences.

2. Host Contests and Giveaways

Engage your audience with contests and giveaways that encourage participation and interaction.

- **Photo Contests**: Host photo contests related to real estate or community themes.
- **Giveaways**: Offer prizes such as gift cards, home décor items, or local services.
- **Entry Requirements**: Encourage participation by asking followers to like, share, or comment on your posts.

3. Collaborate with Influencers

Partner with local influencers or industry experts to reach a broader audience and enhance your credibility.

- **Influencer Partnerships**: Collaborate with influencers who align with your brand and have a following in your target market.
- **Guest Posts**: Invite influencers to contribute guest posts or videos to your social media channels.
- **Joint Campaigns**: Work together on joint social media campaigns or events to maximize reach.

4. Utilize Paid Advertising

Leverage paid advertising options on social media platforms to target specific demographics and geographic areas.

- **Targeted Ads**: Create targeted ads based on factors such as location, age, interests, and behaviors.
- **Ad Formats**: Use various ad formats, including image ads, video ads, and carousel ads, to capture attention and drive engagement.
- **Budget Management**: Set a budget for your ad campaigns and monitor performance to optimize results.

Measuring Success and Adjusting Strategies

To ensure the effectiveness of your social media efforts, regularly measure your performance and adjust your strategies as needed:

1. Track Key Metrics

Monitor key metrics to assess the performance of your social media activities:

- **Engagement**: Track likes, comments, shares, and overall engagement to gauge the effectiveness of your content.
- **Reach and Impressions**: Measure the reach and impressions of your posts to understand how many people are seeing your content.
- **Conversions**: Track conversions such as leads generated, website visits, and inquiries resulting from social media efforts.

2. Analyze Performance

Use analytics tools provided by social media platforms to analyze performance and identify trends:

- **Platform Analytics**: Review insights and analytics available on each social media platform to evaluate performance.
- **Third-Party Tools**: Utilize third-party analytics tools to gain additional insights and track cross-platform performance.
- **Performance Reports**: Create regular performance reports to summarize key metrics and assess progress.

3. Adjust Strategies

Based on your analysis, adjust your social media strategies to improve results:

- **Content Optimization**: Modify your content based on what resonates most with your audience. Experiment with different formats, topics, and posting times.
- **Advertising Adjustments**: Refine your paid advertising campaigns based on performance data. Adjust targeting, ad creatives, and budgets as needed.
- **Engagement Tactics**: Enhance your engagement tactics based on feedback and interaction patterns.

Action Item: Implementing an Effective Social Media Strategy

To implement an effective social media strategy, follow these steps:

Step 1: Define Your Social Media Goals

Determine your social media goals, such as increasing brand awareness, generating leads, or showcasing properties. Set measurable objectives to guide your efforts.

Step 2: Select Platforms and Create Content

Choose the social media platforms that align with your target audience and create a content plan. Develop a mix of property listings, market insights, educational content, and community involvement posts.

Step 3: Engage with Your Audience

Actively engage with your audience by responding to comments, messages, and inquiries. Host contests, collaborate with influencers, and utilize paid advertising to enhance engagement.

Step 4: Measure and Adjust

Track key metrics and analyze performance to assess the effectiveness of your social media efforts. Adjust your strategies based on insights and feedback to continuously improve results.

Executing the Method

Begin by defining your social media goals and selecting the platforms that best suit your target audience. Create a content plan that includes a variety of posts, such as property listings, market insights, and educational content. Actively engage with your audience through timely responses, contests, and collaborations. Utilize paid advertising to reach specific demographics and track key metrics to measure success. Regularly analyze performance and adjust your strategies to optimize results. Implementing these steps will effectively leverage social media to enhance your real estate business and achieve your goals.

Social media is a powerful tool for real estate professionals, offering opportunities to increase visibility, engage with clients, and showcase properties. By selecting the right platforms, creating compelling content, and actively engaging with your audience, you can harness the power of social media to drive business growth and build a strong online presence. Regularly measure your performance and adjust your strategies to ensure continued success in leveraging social media for real estate success.

Action Steps

Define Your Social Media Goals:

- Set clear goals such as increasing brand awareness, generating leads, or showcasing properties. Make these objectives measurable to track progress.

Select the Right Social Media Platforms:

- Choose platforms that align with your target audience. Depending on your business objectives, focus on Facebook, Instagram, LinkedIn, Twitter, or YouTube.

Create Compelling Content:

- Post high-quality photos and videos of properties.
- Share market insights, tips, client testimonials, and community involvement updates.
- Use formats like Stories, Reels, and live virtual open houses to boost engagement.

Engage with Your Audience:

- Respond to comments, messages, and inquiries in a timely and personalized manner.
- Host contests and giveaways to encourage interaction.
- Collaborate with influencers and other industry professionals to extend your reach.

Leverage Paid Advertising:

- Utilize Facebook and Instagram ads to target specific demographics and geographic locations.
- To drive engagement, experiment with different ad formats such as image, video, and carousel ads.

Measure Performance:

- Use platform analytics and third-party tools to track key metrics like engagement, reach, conversions, and website visits.
- Regularly assess your social media performance to understand which content works best.

Analyze and Adjust Strategies:

- Optimize your content based on audience feedback and engagement patterns.
- Refine your paid advertising campaigns based on performance data.
- Adjust posting schedules and content formats to improve overall engagement.

Regularly Evaluate and Refine:

- Continuously measure the effectiveness of your social media efforts and adjust as necessary to optimize your strategy and achieve your goals.

10

Effective Networking Strategies for Real Estate Professionals

Networking is an essential component of a successful real estate career. Building a robust network of industry professionals, clients, and community contacts can open doors to new opportunities, generate leads, and enhance your reputation. In this chapter, we will explore effective networking strategies tailored to real estate professionals, including how to build and maintain valuable connections, leverage networking events, and utilize online tools for optimal networking results.

The Importance of Networking in Real Estate

Networking plays a crucial role in real estate for several reasons:

1. **Lead Generation**: Networking helps generate leads by connecting you with potential clients, referral sources, and industry partners. A well-established network can provide a steady stream of new business opportunities.

2. **Industry Knowledge**: Networking allows you to stay informed about industry trends, market conditions, and best practices. Engaging with other professionals provides insights to enhance your expertise and keep you ahead of the competition.

3. **Reputation Building**: Building a positive reputation within your network can lead to more referrals and recommendations. Demonstrating your professionalism and expertise helps establish trust and credibility.

4. **Partnership Opportunities**: Networking opens doors to potential partnerships with other professionals, such as mortgage brokers, home inspectors, and contractors. These partnerships can lead to mutually beneficial collaborations and increased business opportunities.

5. **Community Engagement**: Networking helps you become more involved in your community. Engaging with local organizations, events, and residents strengthens your presence and fosters positive relationships.

Building and Maintaining Valuable Connections

Effective networking involves more than just exchanging business cards. To build and maintain valuable connections, consider the following strategies:

1. Identify Key Contacts

Start by identifying the key contacts you want to connect with. This includes:

- **Industry Professionals**: Other real estate agents, mortgage brokers, home inspectors, appraisers, and contractors.
- **Potential Clients**: Individuals and families who may be looking to buy or sell property.
- **Local Business Owners**: Owners of businesses in your area who can provide referrals and collaborate on community initiatives.
- **Community Leaders**: Local leaders and influencers who can help you establish credibility and expand your network.

2. Attend Networking Events

Networking events provide opportunities to meet and connect with industry professionals and potential clients. To maximize the benefits of these events:

- **Choose Relevant Events**: Attend events relevant to your industry and target audience. This includes real estate conferences, trade shows, local business mixers, and community events.
- **Prepare Your Elevator Pitch**: Develop a concise and compelling elevator pitch that highlights your expertise, services, and unique selling points. Practice delivering it confidently.

- **Be Approachable**: Engage in conversations, ask questions, and show genuine interest in others. Avoid focusing solely on promoting yourself.
- **Follow Up**: Follow up with the contacts you met after the event. Send personalized emails or LinkedIn requests to continue the conversation and build a relationship.

3. Leverage Online Networking Tools

Online networking tools and platforms offer additional opportunities to connect with industry professionals and potential clients:

- **LinkedIn**: Build and maintain a professional profile on LinkedIn. Connect with industry peers, join relevant groups, and participate in discussions to showcase your expertise.
- **Industry Forums and Groups**: Join online forums and groups related to real estate to engage in discussions, share insights, and connect with other professionals.
- **Social Media**: Utilize social media platforms to engage with your network, share valuable content, and participate in relevant conversations.

4. Offer Value and Support

To build lasting relationships, focus on offering value and support to your network:

- **Share Knowledge**: Provide valuable information, such as market insights, tips, and resources, that can benefit your contacts.

- **Be a Resource**: Offer assistance and support to others in your network, whether it's providing referrals, answering questions, or sharing industry updates.
- **Celebrate Success**: Acknowledge and celebrate the achievements and milestones of your contacts. This fosters goodwill and strengthens your relationships.

5. Join Professional Organizations

Joining professional organizations can enhance your networking efforts and provide additional resources:

- **Local Real Estate Associations**: Become a member of local real estate associations to connect with other professionals and stay informed about industry trends.
- **National Associations**: Join national real estate associations, such as the National Association of Realtors (NAR), to access resources, attend events, and network with a broader audience.
- **Specialty Groups**: Participate in specialty groups or associations related to specific areas of real estate, such as commercial real estate or luxury properties.

Leveraging Networking Events for Maximum Impact

Networking events are valuable opportunities to connect with potential clients, industry peers, and community leaders. To make the most of these events:

1. Set Clear Objectives

Before attending a networking event, set clear objectives for what you want to achieve. This could include:

- **Meeting Specific Contacts**: Identify key individuals you want to connect with and develop a plan to approach them.
- **Generating Leads**: Set a goal for the number of new leads or potential clients you want to acquire.
- **Building Partnerships**: Aim to establish connections with professionals who can become valuable partners or collaborators.

2. Prepare and Plan

Effective preparation and planning can enhance your networking experience:

- **Research Attendees**: If possible, review the list of attendees or participants to identify individuals or companies you want to connect with.
- **Bring Marketing Materials**: Have business cards, brochures, or promotional materials ready to share with potential contacts.
- **Dress Professionally**: Present yourself professionally to make a positive impression.

3. Engage and Connect

During the event, focus on engaging with others and building meaningful connections:

- **Be Genuine**: Approach conversations with a genuine interest in the other person's needs and interests.
- **Listen Actively**: Practice active listening and ask questions to learn more about the other person's background and goals.
- **Follow Up Promptly**: After the event, follow up with the contacts you met to continue the conversation and strengthen the relationship.

4. Host Networking Events

Consider hosting networking events to build and nurture relationships:

- **Organize Events**: Host events such as open houses, seminars, or networking mixers to connect with clients, industry professionals, and community members.
- **Promote Your Event**: Use social media, email marketing, and local advertising to promote your event and attract attendees.
- **Provide Value**: Ensure your event offers value to attendees, such as informative presentations, valuable networking opportunities, or enjoyable experiences.

Utilizing Online Tools and Platforms

Online tools and platforms can complement your in-person networking efforts and expand your reach:

1. LinkedIn

LinkedIn is a powerful tool for professional networking:

- **Optimize Your Profile**: Ensure your LinkedIn profile is complete and up to date with a professional photo, detailed experience, and relevant keywords.
- **Connect Strategically**: Send personalized connection requests to individuals you want to network with, including a brief introduction and reason for connecting.
- **Engage in Groups**: Join LinkedIn groups related to real estate and participate in discussions to share your expertise and connect with others.

2. Industry-Specific Forums

Participate in industry-specific forums and online communities to engage with peers and stay informed:

- **Join Relevant Forums**: Find and join forums related to real estate, such as those focused on market trends, best practices, or niche areas of interest.
- **Contribute to Discussions**: Share your insights, answer questions, and contribute to discussions to build your reputation and connect with others.

3. Social Media

Use social media platforms to enhance your networking efforts:

- **Engage with Followers**: Respond to comments, messages, and inquiries to build relationships with your social media audience.
- **Share Valuable Content**: Post content that provides value to your followers, such as market updates, tips, and success stories.
- **Participate in Conversations**: Join and contribute to conversations related to real estate and your local community.

Building Long-Term Relationships

Effective networking is not just about making initial connections; it's about building and maintaining long-term relationships. To achieve this:

1. Stay in Touch

Maintain regular contact with your network to stay top of mind:

- **Send Updates**: Share periodic updates about your business, achievements, and industry news.
- **Schedule Check-Ins**: Reach out to your contacts periodically to catch up and offer support.
- **Use a CRM System**: Utilize a customer relationship management (CRM) system to track interactions and schedule follow-ups.

2. Provide Value Continuously

Continue to provide value to your network by:

- **Sharing Resources**: Offer valuable resources, such as market reports, industry news, or useful tools.
- **Offering Support**: Be available to assist with any questions, referrals, or advice your contacts may need.
- **Celebrating Milestones**: Recognize and celebrate the achievements and milestones of your contacts, such as promotions, anniversaries, or business successes.

3. Seek Feedback and Collaborate

Collaborate with your network and seek feedback to enhance your relationships:

- **Request Feedback**: Ask for feedback on your services and interactions to understand how you can improve.
- **Collaborate on Projects**: Explore opportunities to collaborate with others on projects, events, or initiatives that benefit both parties.
- **Share Success Stories**: Share success stories and testimonials that highlight the positive outcomes of your collaborations.

Action Item: Implementing an Effective Networking Strategy

To implement an effective networking strategy, follow these steps:

Step 1: Identify Your Networking Goals

Determine your networking goals, such as generating leads, building partnerships, or expanding your industry knowledge. Set specific and measurable objectives to guide your efforts.

Step 2: Develop a Networking Plan

Create a networking plan that includes attending relevant events, leveraging online tools, and engaging with your contacts. Outline your strategies for building and maintaining connections.

Step 3: Execute and Follow Up

Attend networking events, connect with industry professionals, and engage in online communities. Follow up with the contacts you meet and offer value to build and nurture relationships.

Step 4: Evaluate and Adjust

Regularly evaluate the effectiveness of your networking efforts and adjust your strategies as needed. Track key metrics, such as new leads, partnerships, and referrals, to measure success.

Executing the Method

Begin by setting clear networking goals and developing a plan that includes attending relevant events, leveraging online platforms, and offering value to your contacts. Engage in meaningful conversations, follow up with new connections, and maintain regular contact with your network. Use tools like LinkedIn and industry-specific forums to expand your reach and enhance your networking efforts. Regularly assess your progress and adjust your strategies to ensure continued success in building and maintaining valuable relationships.

Conclusion

Effective networking is a cornerstone of success in the real estate industry. Building and maintaining valuable connections, leveraging networking events and online tools, and offering continuous value can enhance your reputation, generate leads, and create new opportunities. Implementing a strategic networking approach will help you establish a strong network of industry professionals, clients, and community contacts, ultimately driving your real estate career forward.

Action Steps

Identify Networking Goals:

- Set specific goals, such as generating leads, building partnerships, or expanding industry knowledge.
- Define measurable objectives to track your progress.

Build and Maintain Valuable Connections:

- Focus on connecting with key contacts such as industry professionals (mortgage brokers, inspectors), potential clients, local business owners, and community leaders.
- Attend relevant events (real estate conferences, mixers, local community events) to expand your network.

Prepare for Networking Events:

- Develop a compelling elevator pitch and prepare marketing materials (business cards, brochures).
- Set clear objectives for each event, such as meeting specific contacts or generating leads.

Leverage Online Networking Tools:

- Optimize your LinkedIn profile and engage in relevant LinkedIn groups.
- Join industry-specific forums and social media platforms to connect with peers and stay informed.

Offer Value to Your Network:

- Share industry insights, resources, and advice with your network.
- Be a resource to others by offering referrals, answering questions, or providing industry updates.

Host Networking Events:

- Organize open houses, seminars, or mixers to build relationships and showcase your expertise.
- Promote events through social media, email marketing, and local advertising.

Follow Up and Maintain Long-Term Relationships:

- Send regular updates and check-ins to stay top of mind.
- Use a CRM system to track contacts and schedule follow-ups.
- Celebrate milestones, such as promotions or business successes, to show appreciation.

Evaluate Networking Efforts:

- Regularly assess the effectiveness of your networking strategies using key metrics like new leads, partnerships, and referrals.
- Adjust your approach based on feedback and results to improve outcomes.

11

Crafting Effective Referral Programs and Incentives

Referral programs are a cornerstone of growth for real estate professionals, leveraging existing client relationships to generate new leads and expand business opportunities. Implementing a well-designed referral program rewards loyal clients and attracts potential clients who are likely to value your services. This chapter will delve into the intricacies of developing and executing effective referral programs and incentives, covering how to design your program, communicate it effectively, and measure its success.

The Power of Referral Programs

Referral programs harness the power of word-of-mouth marketing, which is one of the most credible and influential forms of advertising. Clients who refer others to your services are advocating for you and validating your expertise and trustworthiness. Referral programs offer several benefits:

1. **Cost-Effective Marketing**: Referral programs are often more cost-effective than traditional advertising. Instead of spending on ads, you invest in rewarding existing clients, which can be more impactful.

2. **High-Quality Leads**: Referrals tend to result in high-quality leads, as they come from trusted sources. Referred clients are more likely to convert into customers and have a higher lifetime value.

3. **Increased Client Retention**: Implementing a referral program can enhance client loyalty and retention. Clients who participate in referral programs feel more valued and are more likely to continue using your services.

4. **Enhanced Reputation**: A successful referral program can boost your reputation by generating positive word-of-mouth. Satisfied clients sharing their experiences contribute to building your brand's credibility.

Designing Your Referral Program

Creating an effective referral program requires careful planning and consideration. Follow these steps to design a program that aligns with your business goals and resonates with your clients:

1. Define Your Objectives

Clarify what you want to achieve with your referral program:

- **Lead Generation**: Focus on generating new leads and expanding your client base.
- **Client Retention**: Aim to strengthen relationships with existing clients and enhance their loyalty.
- **Brand Awareness**: Use referrals to increase brand visibility and reach new audiences.

2. Determine Incentives

Choose incentives that will motivate your clients to participate in the referral program. Consider the following options:

- **Monetary Rewards**: Offer cash bonuses or discounts on future transactions as rewards for successful referrals.
- **Gift Cards**: Provide gift cards to popular retailers or restaurants as a token of appreciation.
- **Exclusive Services**: Offer access to exclusive services, such as complimentary consultations or premium market reports.

- **Charitable Donations**: Donate to a charity of the client's choice in their name as a reward for successful referrals.

3. Establish Referral Criteria

Clearly define the criteria for what constitutes a successful referral. This may include:

- **Qualified Leads**: Ensure referrals meet specific qualifications, such as being serious buyers or sellers.
- **Conversion Requirements**: Specify that the referral must result in a closed transaction or signed agreement to qualify for rewards.

4. Create a Referral Process

Develop a straightforward and easy-to-follow referral process:

- **Referral Form**: Design a referral form or online submission system where clients can provide information about their referrals.
- **Tracking System**: Implement a tracking system to monitor and manage referrals, ensuring no referrals are overlooked.
- **Communication**: Clearly communicate the referral process to clients, including how they can refer others and track the status of their referrals.

5. Promote Your Referral Program

Effectively promote your referral program to ensure clients are aware of it and motivated to participate:

- **Email Campaigns**: Send targeted email campaigns to your existing clients, highlighting the benefits and details of the referral program.
- **Social Media**: Use social media platforms to announce and promote your referral program. Share success stories and testimonials to encourage participation.
- **Website**: Feature information about the referral program prominently on your website, including a dedicated page with details and a referral submission form.
- **In-Person Communication**: Discuss the referral program with clients during meetings, open houses, or other interactions.

Executing Your Referral Program

Successful execution of your referral program involves managing the program effectively, ensuring timely rewards, and maintaining clear communication with clients:

1. Track Referrals

Monitor and manage referrals to ensure they are tracked accurately and efficiently:

- **Referral Tracking System**: Utilize a CRM or referral management system to track and record referral submissions, progress, and outcomes.

- **Regular Updates**: Provide regular updates to clients about the status of their referrals and any rewards they may be eligible for.

2. Reward Timely

Ensure rewards are distributed promptly to maintain client satisfaction and motivation:

- **Reward Processing**: Process and distribute rewards as soon as a referral meets the established criteria. Avoid delays that could impact client satisfaction.
- **Personalized Thank-You**: Send personalized thank-you notes or messages to clients who have successfully referred others, expressing appreciation for their support.

3. Maintain Communication

Keep open lines of communication with clients throughout the referral process:

- **Acknowledge Referrals**: Acknowledge receipt of referrals and provide updates on the status of the referred client.
- **Feedback**: Request feedback from clients about their experience with the referral program and make improvements based on their input.

Measuring the Success of Your Referral Program

Assessing the effectiveness of your referral program is essential to understanding its impact and identifying areas for improvement:

1. Track Key Metrics

Monitor key performance indicators (KPIs) to evaluate the success of your referral program:

- **Number of Referrals**: Track the total number of referrals received and converted into clients.
- **Conversion Rate**: Measure the percentage of referrals that result in successful transactions or new clients.
- **Client Retention Rate**: Assess whether clients who participate in the referral program show higher retention rates compared to those who do not.
- **Return on Investment (ROI)**: Calculate your referral program's ROI by comparing the incentives' costs with the revenue generated from new clients.

2. Analyze Feedback

Gather and analyze feedback from clients and referrals to gain insights into the program's effectiveness:

- **Client Feedback**: Collect feedback from clients about their experience with the referral program and any suggestions for improvement.

- **Referral Experience**: Obtain feedback from referred clients about their experience with your services and the referral process.

3. Adjust and Improve

Based on your analysis, adjust to enhance the referral program:

- **Revise Incentives**: Modify incentives based on client preferences and feedback to ensure they remain attractive and motivating.
- **Refine Processes**: Streamline the referral process and address any issues or bottlenecks hindering the program's success.
- **Enhance Promotion**: Increase promotional efforts to boost awareness and participation in the referral program.

Action Item: Implementing a Referral Program

To implement a successful referral program, follow these steps:

Step 1: Design the Program

Define your objectives, determine incentives, establish referral criteria, and create a referral process. Develop promotional materials and strategies to communicate the program to your clients.

Step 2: Execute and Track

Launch the referral program, ensuring a smooth execution and tracking system. Reward clients promptly and maintain clear communication throughout the referral process.

Step 3: Measure and Improve

Monitor key metrics, gather feedback, and analyze the program's effectiveness. Make necessary adjustments to improve the program and enhance its impact.

Executing the Method

Design a referral program that aligns with your objectives and client preferences. Implement the program with effective tracking and timely rewards. Promote the program through various channels to maximize client participation. Regularly measure the program's success and adjust based on feedback and performance metrics. Following these steps will create a successful referral program that drives new business and strengthens client relationships.

Referral programs are a powerful tool for real estate professionals, providing a cost-effective and impactful way to generate new leads and build client loyalty. By designing a well-structured referral program, effectively promoting it, and measuring its success, you can leverage the power of client referrals to enhance your business growth and reputation. Implementing a successful referral program will not only reward your loyal clients but also attract high-quality leads and contribute to the overall success of your real estate practice.

Action Steps

Design Your Referral Program:

- **Define Objectives:** Decide on the program's goals (e.g., lead generation, client retention, or brand awareness).
- **Determine Incentives:** Choose attractive rewards, such as monetary incentives, gift cards, exclusive services, or charitable donations.
- **Establish Referral Criteria:** Define what constitutes a successful referral, including qualified leads and conversion requirements.
- **Create a Referral Process:** Develop a simple and efficient process for clients to submit referrals and track their status.

Promote Your Referral Program:

- Use email campaigns, social media, and your website to inform clients about the program.
- Discuss the program in person during meetings or open houses to generate awareness.

Track and Manage Referrals:

- Implement a CRM or tracking system to monitor referrals and ensure none are missed.
- Provide regular updates to clients about the status of their referrals.

Reward Timely:

- Process rewards quickly after a successful referral to maintain client satisfaction.
- Send personalized thank-you notes or messages to acknowledge the client's contribution.

Maintain Clear Communication:

- Acknowledge referrals as they are received and keep referrers informed of the progress.
- Collect feedback from both referrers and referred clients to evaluate the program's effectiveness.

Measure Success:

- Track key metrics like the number of referrals, conversion rates, client retention, and ROI to assess the program's success.
- Gather feedback from clients and referral sources to identify areas for improvement.

Adjust and Improve:

- Modify incentives, refine the referral process, and enhance promotional efforts based on feedback and performance analysis.

Execute the Program:

- Launch your referral program, ensuring a smooth execution and effective tracking system.
- Regularly evaluate the program's impact and adjust strategies to improve results.

12

Engaging with Local Businesses

E ngaging with local businesses is a strategic move for real estate professionals looking to expand their network, build community relationships, and generate new leads. By fostering partnerships with local businesses, realtors can tap into a broader network, enhance their visibility, and create mutually beneficial opportunities. In this chapter, we'll explore the importance of engaging with local businesses, developing these relationships, and leveraging these connections to grow your real estate practice.

The Importance of Local Business Engagement

Engaging with local businesses offers several advantages for real estate professionals:

1. **Networking Opportunities**: Local businesses often have established relationships with community

members. You can expand your network and connect with potential clients by partnering with them.

2. **Mutual Referrals**: Establishing a referral network with local businesses can lead to a steady stream of referrals, as business owners may refer their customers to you and vice versa.

3. **Community Integration**: Being actively involved with local businesses integrates you into the community, enhancing your reputation and positioning you as a local expert.

4. **Increased Visibility**: Collaborating with local businesses can increase your visibility in the community, as your name and brand become associated with trusted local establishments.

5. **Enhanced Credibility**: Partnerships with respected local businesses can boost your credibility, as clients may view you as a reliable and well-connected professional.

Developing Relationships with Local Businesses

Building relationships with local businesses requires a thoughtful approach. Here's how to develop and nurture these connections:

1. Identify Potential Business Partners

Start by identifying local businesses that align with your values and target market. Consider businesses your clients might frequent or that complement your real estate services. Some examples include:

- **Home Improvement Stores**: Partnering with home improvement stores can be beneficial, as they cater to homeowners and potential homebuyers.
- **Interior Designers**: Collaborating with interior designers can provide value to your clients, especially those looking to stage or renovate their homes.
- **Mortgage Brokers**: Building a relationship with mortgage brokers can help streamline the homebuying process for your clients and lead to mutual referrals.
- **Local Restaurants and Cafes**: Engaging with popular local dining spots can increase your visibility among community members and provide opportunities for hosting events.
- **Law Firms and Accountants**: Professionals in legal and financial fields can refer clients who need real estate services, such as estate planning or tax advice related to property transactions.

2. Approach with Value in Mind

When contacting local businesses, focus on how your partnership can benefit them. Consider the following strategies:

- **Cross-Promotions**: Offer to promote their business to your clients and network in exchange for them doing the same for you. For example, you could feature their services in your newsletter, and they could display your business cards or brochures in their store.
- **Exclusive Offers**: Propose exclusive discounts or offers for clients referred by your business. This can create a win-win situation where both businesses gain new customers.

- **Event Collaboration**: Suggest co-hosting events, such as workshops or community gatherings, where both businesses can showcase their offerings and engage with potential clients.

3. Attend Local Business Events

Participating in local business events is an excellent way to network and build relationships:

- **Chamber of Commerce Meetings**: Join your local Chamber of Commerce and attend their meetings and events. These gatherings are ideal for meeting other business owners and discussing potential collaborations.
- **Business Networking Groups**: Become a member of local business networking groups, where you can regularly interact with other professionals and explore partnership opportunities.
- **Community Events**: Attend or sponsor community events, such as festivals, charity fundraisers, or local fairs, where you can connect with both business owners and potential clients.

4. Offer Your Expertise

Position yourself as a valuable resource by offering your real estate expertise to local businesses:

- **Real Estate Seminars**: Host seminars or workshops for business owners and their employees on topics like commercial real estate trends, property investment, or homebuying tips.

- **Consulting Services**: Provide consulting services to local businesses looking to expand, relocate, or invest in property. Your guidance can help them make informed decisions and strengthen your relationship.
- **Content Collaboration**: Collaborate with local businesses on content creation, such as blog posts, social media content, or videos that provide value to their audience while showcasing your expertise.

Leveraging Local Business Relationships

Once you've established relationships with local businesses, it's important to leverage these connections to grow your real estate practice:

1. Create a Local Business Directory

Develop a directory of trusted local businesses to share with your clients. This directory could include home improvement stores, contractors, landscapers, interior designers, and other service providers your clients might need during their home buying or selling journey. By offering this resource, you position yourself as a well-connected and helpful realtor, which can enhance client satisfaction and loyalty.

2. Co-Host Client Events

Collaborate with local businesses to co-host client events that provide value and entertainment:

- **Homeownership Workshops**: Partner with a mortgage broker, interior designer, and home improvement store to host a workshop on homeownership, covering topics like financing, decorating, and DIY home projects.

- **Community Socials**: Team up with a local restaurant or café to host a community social event where clients can network, enjoy good food, and learn more about your services.
- **Charity Fundraisers**: Collaborate with local businesses to host a charity event, such as a silent auction or fundraising dinner. Not only does this give back to the community, but it also strengthens your relationships with local businesses and clients.

3. Engage on Social Media

Leverage social media to highlight your partnerships with local businesses:

- **Feature Collaborations**: Share posts about your collaborations with local businesses, such as co-hosted events, joint promotions, or successful client referrals.
- **Tag and Mention**: Tag local businesses in your social media posts and mention them in your stories to show support and increase their visibility.
- **Content Sharing**: Share content from local businesses that could interest your audience, such as tips from a home improvement store or an interior designer's latest project.

4. Implement a Local Business Referral Program

Develop a referral program specifically for local businesses, encouraging them to refer their customers to you in exchange for incentives:

- **Referral Rewards**: Offer incentives such as gift cards, discounts on services, or donations to a charity of the business's choice for successful referrals.
- **Business Partnership Benefits**: Provide additional benefits for businesses that regularly refer clients to you, such as featuring them prominently in your business directory, promoting their services to your network, or offering them exclusive deals on their real estate needs.

5. Sponsor Local Events and Initiatives

Sponsoring local events and initiatives can further strengthen your ties to the community and local businesses:

- **Community Sponsorships**: Sponsor local sports teams, school events, or community festivals. This increases your brand visibility and shows your commitment to the community.
- **Business Initiatives**: Support local business initiatives, such as "shop local" campaigns or small business expos, by sponsoring or participating in these events.
- **Public Relations**: Work with local media outlets to highlight your involvement in community events and business partnerships, further boosting your reputation as a community-focused real estate professional.

Action Item: Engaging with Local Businesses

To effectively engage with local businesses and leverage these relationships, follow these steps:

Step 1: Identify and Approach

Identify local businesses that align with your target market and approach them with value-driven proposals for collaboration.

Step 2: Develop Relationships

Build and nurture relationships by attending local business events, offering your expertise, and collaborating on cross-promotions and events.

Step 3: Leverage Partnerships

Leverage these partnerships by creating a local business directory, co-hosting client events, engaging on social media, and implementing a referral program.

Step 4: Expand Community Involvement

Further strengthen your community ties by sponsoring local events and initiatives, supporting business campaigns, and engaging in public relations efforts.

Executing the Method

Start by identifying local businesses that align with your values and target market. Approach these businesses with value-driven proposals and develop relationships through consistent engagement and collaboration. Leverage these partnerships to grow your real estate practice by creating a local business directory, co-hosting events, and promoting each other's services. Expand your community involvement by sponsoring local events and initiatives, enhancing your reputation and visibility as a trusted local expert.

Engaging with local businesses is a strategic way to build your network, enhance your visibility, and grow your real estate practice. Developing and nurturing relationships with local businesses can create mutually beneficial partnerships that generate new leads, strengthen community ties, and boost your credibility. Implementing the strategies outlined in this chapter will help you establish yourself as a key player in your local business ecosystem, ultimately contributing to your long-term success in real estate.

Action Steps

Identify Potential Business Partners:

- Look for local businesses that align with your target market, such as home improvement stores, interior designers, mortgage brokers, restaurants, and law firms.
- Consider businesses that complement your real estate services and provide value to your clients.

Approach with Value:

- Propose mutually beneficial partnerships like cross-promotions, exclusive offers, or event collaborations.
- Focus on how the partnership can benefit both businesses by offering value to their customers.

Attend Local Business Events:

- Join local business networking groups, attend Chamber of Commerce meetings, and participate in community events to meet potential business partners.
- Use these events to build relationships and discuss collaboration opportunities.

Offer Your Expertise:

- Position yourself as a valuable resource by hosting real estate seminars for local businesses and offering consulting services to help them with property-related decisions.
- Collaborate on content creation (e.g., blog posts, social media content) to provide value to their audience while showcasing your expertise.

Leverage Local Business Relationships:

- Create a local business directory to share with your clients, featuring trusted businesses you collaborate with.
- Co-host client events, like homeownership workshops or community socials, with local businesses to strengthen your partnerships and engage with clients.

Engage on Social Media:

- Highlight your local business collaborations on social media, tagging businesses in posts and sharing their content with your audience.

- Use your social media platforms to increase visibility for your business and your local business partners.

Implement a Local Business Referral Program:

- Develop a referral program specifically for local businesses, offering incentives such as gift cards or donations to charities for successful referrals.
- Provide additional benefits to businesses that consistently refer clients to you, such as promotions or discounts on real estate services.

Sponsor Local Events and Initiatives:

- Sponsor local community events, such as sports teams or charity fundraisers, to increase your visibility and demonstrate your commitment to the community.
- Support "shop local" initiatives or small business expos to further integrate your real estate services within the local business ecosystem.

Measure Success and Build Relationships:

- Regularly assess the success of your business partnerships through feedback and referral tracking.
- Continue to build relationships by attending events, hosting joint initiatives, and providing ongoing support to local businesses.

13

Hosting Community Events and Workshops

osting community events and workshops is a powerful strategy for real estate professionals looking to engage with potential clients, build relationships, and establish themselves as trusted experts in their local markets. These events offer an opportunity to connect with your community on a personal level, showcase your knowledge, and provide valuable information to attendees. In this chapter, we'll explore the benefits of hosting community events, how to plan and execute successful events, and how to leverage these opportunities to grow your real estate business.

The Benefits of Hosting Community Events and Workshops

Organizing and hosting community events can yield several significant benefits for real estate professionals:

1. **Enhanced Visibility**: Hosting events increases your visibility within the community, positioning you as an active and engaged local expert.
2. **Relationship Building**: Community events offer a platform for building relationships with potential clients in a relaxed, non-salesy environment.
3. **Trust and Credibility**: Providing valuable information and resources through workshops enhances your credibility and helps build trust with attendees.
4. **Lead Generation**: Events attract potential clients who are interested in real estate, creating opportunities for lead generation and future business.
5. **Community Involvement**: Being involved in community events demonstrates your commitment to the local area, which can strengthen your reputation and brand.

Planning a Successful Community Event or Workshop

Careful planning and attention to detail are essential to host a successful community event or workshop. Here's how to get started:

1. Define Your Objectives

Before planning your event, it's important to define your objectives. Consider what you want to achieve:

- **Lead Generation**: Attract potential clients who may be interested in buying or selling a property.
- **Brand Awareness**: Increase awareness of your real estate business and services within the community.
- **Educational Outreach**: Provide valuable information and resources to attendees, positioning yourself as an expert.
- **Networking**: Build relationships with local businesses, community leaders, and potential clients.

2. Choose the Right Event Type

Select an event type that aligns with your objectives and will resonate with your target audience. Some popular options include:

- **Homebuyer Workshops**: Educate first-time homebuyers about the homebuying process, financing options, and market trends.
- **Seller Seminars**: Provide insights for homeowners looking to sell, including tips on staging, pricing, and marketing their property.
- **Community Socials**: Host casual social events, such as a neighborhood barbecue or coffee meet-and-greet, to connect with local residents in a relaxed setting.
- **Real Estate Market Updates**: Offer a presentation on current market conditions, trends, and forecasts to keep your audience informed.
- **Charity Fundraisers**: Organize an event that supports a local cause or charity, demonstrating your commitment to the community.

3. Select a Venue

Choose a venue that is convenient, accessible, and suitable for the type of event you're hosting:

- **Local Community Centers**: Community centers are often available for public events and provide a central location for attendees.
- **Partnering Businesses**: Consider hosting your event at a local business, such as a café, restaurant, or retail store, which can also help cross-promote the event.
- **Outdoor Spaces**: Consider using an outdoor space, such as a park or public square, for larger or more casual events.
- **Your Office**: If you have a spacious and professional office, hosting the event there can provide a more personal touch.

4. Develop Event Content

The content of your event is crucial to its success. Ensure it is informative, engaging, and relevant to your audience:

- **Presentation Materials**: Prepare slides, handouts, or other materials that provide valuable information and support your presentation.
- **Interactive Elements**: Include interactive elements, such as Q&A sessions, group discussions, or hands-on activities, to keep attendees engaged.
- **Guest Speakers**: Invite guest speakers, such as mortgage brokers, home inspectors, or interior designers,

to provide additional expertise and value to your audience.

5. Promote Your Event

Effective promotion is key to attracting attendees. Utilize multiple channels to spread the word:

- **Email Marketing**: Send targeted emails to your contact list, including past clients, leads, and community members, with details about the event.
- **Social Media**: Promote the event on your social media platforms, using eye-catching visuals and engaging captions to generate interest.
- **Flyers and Posters**: Distribute flyers and posters in high-traffic areas, such as local businesses, community centers, and schools.
- **Partner Promotions**: Collaborate with local businesses, organizations, or community groups to promote the event to their audiences.
- **Event Listings**: To reach a broader audience, list your event on local event websites, community calendars, and real estate platforms.

6. Prepare for the Event

Ensure everything is in place for a smooth and successful event:

- **Event Agenda**: Create a detailed agenda outlining the schedule, topics to be covered, and any guest speakers or activities.

- **Materials and Supplies**: Prepare all necessary materials, such as presentation slides, handouts, name tags, and refreshments.
- **Technology Setup**: Test all technology, including microphones, projectors, and Wi-Fi, to avoid any technical issues during the event.
- **Registration Process**: Set up a registration process, either online or on-site, to manage attendee sign-ups and track attendance.

Executing a Successful Community Event or Workshop

On the day of the event, focus on delivering a memorable and impactful experience for your attendees:

1. Welcome Attendees

Make a positive first impression by warmly welcoming attendees as they arrive:

- **Greeting**: Personally greet each attendee, introducing yourself and providing a brief event overview.
- **Check-In**: Ensure the check-in process is smooth and organized, with name tags and materials ready for attendees.
- **Networking**: Encourage attendees to mingle and network before the event starts, creating a friendly and engaging atmosphere.

2. Deliver Valuable Content

During the event, focus on delivering informative and engaging content:

- **Presentation**: Present your content clearly and confidently, using visuals and examples to illustrate key points.
- **Engagement**: Keep the audience engaged by asking questions, encouraging participation, and addressing any queries or concerns.
- **Relevance**: Tailor your content to the needs and interests of your audience, ensuring they leave with valuable insights.

3. Facilitate Interaction

Create opportunities for attendees to interact with you and each other:

- **Q&A Sessions**: Allocate time for Q&A sessions where attendees can ask questions and receive personalized advice.
- **Group Activities**: Include group activities or discussions that encourage attendees to share their experiences and learn from each other.
- **Networking Opportunities**: Provide time for networking after the event, allowing attendees to connect with you and other participants.

4. Collect Feedback

After the event, gather feedback to assess its success and identify areas for improvement:

- **Feedback Forms**: Distribute feedback forms or surveys to attendees, asking for their thoughts on the content, format, and overall experience.
- **Follow-Up Conversations**: Engage in follow-up conversations with attendees to gain more detailed insights and build relationships.
- **Analyze Feedback**: Review the feedback collected to identify what worked well and what could be improved for future events.

Leveraging Community Events to Grow Your Business

Hosting community events and workshops is just the beginning. To maximize the impact of these events on your real estate business, consider the following strategies:

1. Build a Contact List

Use your event as an opportunity to build and expand your contact list:

- **Sign-Up Sheets**: Encourage attendees to sign up for your newsletter or mailing list during the event.
- **Business Cards**: Collect business cards from attendees and follow up with personalized emails or calls.

- **Social Media Connections**: Connect with attendees on social media platforms, continuing the conversation and building your online network.

2. Follow Up with Attendees

Effective follow-up is essential to converting event attendees into clients:

- **Thank You Emails**: Send personalized thank-you emails to attendees expressing appreciation for their participation.
- **Resource Sharing**: Share additional resources, such as articles, guides, or market reports, related to the event topic.
- **Consultation Offers**: Offer free consultations or follow-up meetings to discuss attendees' real estate needs in more detail.

3. Share Event Highlights

Leverage the success of your event by sharing highlights and takeaways with a broader audience:

- **Social Media Posts**: Share photos, videos, and key insights from the event on your social media platforms.
- **Blog Posts**: Write a blog post recapping the event, including quotes from guest speakers and feedback from attendees.
- **Email Newsletters**: Include event highlights in your next email newsletter and a call-to-action for readers to contact you for more information.

4. Plan Future Events

Based on the success of your event, start planning future community events and workshops:

- **Regular Events**: To maintain engagement with your audience, consider hosting regular events, such as quarterly market updates or annual homebuyer seminars.
- **Collaborations**: Explore opportunities for collaboration with other local businesses, organizations, or real estate professionals to expand your reach.
- **Continuous Improvement**: Use feedback from previous events to refine your approach, making each event more successful than the last.

Action Item: Hosting a Community Event

To successfully host a community event or workshop, follow these steps:

Step 1: Plan Your Event

Define your objectives, choose the right event type, select a suitable venue, and develop engaging content. Promote the event through multiple channels to attract attendees.

Step 2: Execute with Excellence

On the day of the event, welcome attendees, deliver valuable content, facilitate interaction, and collect feedback to ensure a successful experience.

Step 3: Leverage the Event

After the event, build your contact list, follow up with attendees, share event highlights, and start planning your next event to keep the momentum going.

Hosting community events and workshops is an effective way to engage with your local audience, build relationships, and grow your real estate business. You can create lasting impressions and generate new opportunities by providing valuable information, fostering connections, and positioning yourself as a trusted expert. With careful planning, execution, and follow-up, these events can become a cornerstone of your real estate marketing strategy, helping you achieve long-term success.

Action Steps

Define Event Objectives:

- Identify your goals for the event, such as lead generation, brand awareness, educational outreach, or networking.
- Set measurable objectives to track the success of your event.

Choose the Right Event Type:

- Select an event that aligns with your objectives and resonates with your target audience, such as homebuyer workshops, seller seminars, or community socials.
- Consider events that provide valuable insights and create a relaxed environment for building relationships.

Select a Venue:

- Choose a venue that is accessible, convenient, and suitable for the event type, such as community centers, local businesses, or outdoor spaces.
- Consider venues that can help cross-promote the event, like local cafés or restaurants.

Develop Engaging Content:

- Prepare presentations, materials, and interactive elements to keep attendees engaged.
- Consider inviting guest speakers like mortgage brokers or home inspectors to add value and expertise to your event.

Promote the Event:

- Use email campaigns, social media posts, flyers, and local business partnerships to spread the word.
- List your event on community calendars and real estate platforms to maximize reach.

Prepare for the Event:

- Create a detailed agenda, prepare necessary materials (slides, handouts, name tags), and test any technology beforehand.
- Set up a smooth registration process for attendees, either online or on-site.

Welcome and Engage Attendees:

- Greet attendees warmly and encourage networking before the event starts.
- Present valuable information and facilitate interactive sessions during the event, such as Q&A or group discussions.

Follow Up After the Event:

- Send personalized thank-you emails to attendees, share additional resources, and offer consultations to discuss their real estate needs.
- Use the event as an opportunity to expand your contact list, collecting emails and business cards for future outreach.

Leverage Event Highlights:

- Share photos, videos, and key takeaways from the event on social media, blog posts, and email newsletters.
- Use the event content to further engage your audience and attract new clients.

Plan Future Events:

- Plan regular events to maintain ongoing engagement with your audience.
- Collaborate with local businesses or real estate professionals to expand the reach of future events.

14

Engaging with Local Businesses

E ngaging with local businesses is a highly effective strategy for real estate professionals to expand their sphere of influence, build valuable relationships, and enhance their community presence. By collaborating with local businesses, realtors can tap into new networks, gain referrals, and establish themselves as integral members of the local community. This chapter will explore the benefits of engaging with local businesses, how to establish and maintain these relationships, and specific strategies to create mutually beneficial partnerships.

The Benefits of Engaging with Local Businesses

Partnering with local businesses offers several advantages that can significantly impact your real estate career:

1. **Referral Opportunities**: Local businesses often have established customer bases and networks. You

can tap into these networks for potential client referrals by building relationships with them.

1. **Enhanced Credibility**: Associating with respected local businesses can enhance your credibility and reputation within the community, as you become seen as a trusted partner.

2. **Increased Visibility**: Collaboration with businesses can provide additional platforms to promote your services, such as through co-hosted events, joint marketing efforts, or in-store promotions.

3. **Community Integration**: Working with local businesses helps you integrate more deeply into the community, fostering a sense of connection and loyalty among potential clients.

4. **Support for Local Economy**: By supporting and collaborating with local businesses, you contribute to the growth and sustainability of the local economy, which can enhance your reputation as a community-focused realtor.

Establishing Relationships with Local Businesses

Building strong relationships with local businesses requires a strategic approach, focusing on mutual benefits and long-term collaboration. Here's how to get started:

1. Identify Potential Partners

Start by identifying local businesses that align with your brand values and target market. Consider businesses that:

- **Share a Similar Client Base**: Focus on businesses that cater to the same demographic as your real estate services, such as home improvement stores, interior designers, mortgage brokers, or moving companies.

- **Complement Your Services**: Look for businesses whose services naturally complement real estate, such as home staging companies, landscaping firms, or property management services.
- **Have a Strong Community Presence**: Consider well-known and respected businesses within the community, as their endorsement can enhance your credibility.

2. Initiate Contact

Once you've identified potential partners, the next step is to reach out and initiate contact:

- **Personal Introduction**: Visit the business in person to introduce yourself and express your interest in collaborating. Face-to-face meetings can help establish a personal connection and demonstrate your commitment.
- **Offer Value First**: When initiating contact, focus on how you can add value to their business. This could be through referring clients, co-hosting events, or offering real estate market insights that might interest their customers.
- **Follow Up**: If your initial contact doesn't lead to immediate collaboration, follow up with a thank-you note or email to keep the conversation going and reinforce your interest.

3. Build Trust and Rapport

Building a successful partnership requires trust and rapport, which can be developed over time through consistent and positive interactions:

- **Regular Communication**: Keep in touch with your business partners regularly, whether through meetings, phone calls, or emails, to maintain a strong relationship.
- **Deliver on Promises**: Ensure you follow through on any promises or commitments made during your initial discussions. Reliability is key to building trust.
- **Provide Mutual Support**: Support their business endeavors. This could include attending their events, promoting their services on social media, or referring clients.

Strategies for Engaging with Local Businesses

Engaging with local businesses can lead to successful collaborations in several ways. Below are some strategies to consider:

1. Co-Hosting Events

One of the most effective ways to engage with local businesses is by co-hosting events. This not only provides an opportunity to connect with potential clients but also strengthens your relationship with the business partner:

- **Homebuyer Seminars**: Partner with a mortgage broker or home inspector to host a seminar on the homebuying process, providing valuable information to attendees while showcasing both of your services.
- **Community Fairs**: Collaborate with local businesses to organize a community fair, where each business sets up a booth to offer services, advice, or products to attendees.
- **Charity Events**: Join forces with a local business to host a charity event, such as a fundraising dinner or charity run, which can attract a large audience and demonstrate your commitment to the community.
- **Open Houses**: Partner with local interior designers or home staging companies to co-host open house events, where they can showcase their services while you present the property.

2. Cross-Promotions

Cross-promotions are a simple yet effective way to engage with local businesses and mutually benefit from each other's customer base:

- **Discounts and Offers**: Create joint promotions where local business clients receive a discount on your services and vice versa. For example, a moving company might offer a discount to your clients while you offer a referral discount to their customers who need real estate services.
- **Gift Baskets or Welcome Kits**: Partner with local businesses to create gift baskets or welcome kits for new homeowners. Include items such as gift cards,

coupons, small products from local shops, and information about your real estate services.

- **Social Media Shoutouts**: Promote each other's businesses on social media by sharing posts, tagging each other in updates, or running joint social media campaigns.

- **Feature in Newsletters**: Include a feature about the local business in your email newsletter, highlighting their services and special offers. In return, they can feature your real estate services in their communication channels.

3. Referral Networks

Establishing a referral network with local businesses can be a powerful way to generate leads and expand your client base:

- **Formal Referral Agreements**: Create formal referral agreements where you agree to refer clients to each other. For example, you could agree with a local home staging company to refer clients to each other whenever your services are needed.

- **Informal Referrals**: Encourage informal referrals by regularly communicating with your business partners about potential client needs. For example, if a local business owner knows someone looking to buy or sell a home, they can refer them to you, and you can do the same for them.

- **Referral Rewards**: Offer incentives or rewards for businesses that refer clients to you. This could be a commission, a gift, or a service exchange that benefits both parties.

4. Supporting Local Business Initiatives

Another way to engage with local businesses is by support-ing their initiatives and becoming an active participant in the community:

- **Sponsor Local Events**: Sponsor or co-sponsor events hosted by local businesses, such as community festivals, holiday celebrations, or business expos. Your sponsorship can provide valuable exposure while showing your support for the community.
- **Participate in Local Markets**: Get involved in local markets, such as farmers' markets or art fairs, by set-ting up a booth or sponsoring the event. This allows you to engage directly with community members and local business owners.
- **Join Local Business Associations**: Become a member of local business associations or cham-bers of commerce. These organizations often host networking events, workshops, and other business opportunities to connect and collaborate.

Case Studies: Successful Engagements with Local Businesses

To illustrate the effectiveness of engaging with local busi-nesses, let's explore a few case studies:

Case Study 1: Real Estate Agent and Interior Designer Partnership

A real estate agent in a suburban area partnered with a local interior designer to offer free home staging consultations for clients selling their homes. The interior designer would provide initial staging advice at no cost, and if the homeowner decided to use the designer's services, the real estate agent would receive a referral fee. This partnership not only resulted in quicker home sales but also strengthened the agent's relationships with clients and increased referrals from the designer.

Case Study 2: Realtor and Local Coffee Shop Collaboration

A realtor teamed up with a popular local coffee shop to create a "Welcome to the Neighborhood" program. New homeowners received a gift card to the coffee shop, and in return, the coffee shop featured the realtor's business cards and flyers at the counter. This collaboration helped the realtor build a positive reputation in the community and brought new customers to the coffee shop.

Case Study 3: Community Charity Event Co-Hosted by Multiple Businesses

Several local businesses, including a real estate agency, a moving company, and a home improvement store, collaborated to host a charity event benefiting a local food bank. Each business contributed resources like space, products, and marketing efforts. The event was a huge success, drawing hundreds of attendees, raising significant funds for the charity, and boosting the visibility and reputation of all participating businesses.

Action Item: Engaging with Local Businesses

To effectively engage with local businesses, follow these steps:

Step 1: Identify Potential Partners

Research and identify local businesses that align with your brand, share a similar client base, or offer complementary services.

Step 2: Initiate Contact and Build Relationships

Reach out to potential partners, offer value first, and work on building trust and rapport through consistent communication and mutual support.

Step 3: Collaborate on Initiatives

To create mutually beneficial partnerships, engage in joint initiatives such as co-hosting events, cross-promotions, and referral networks.

Engaging with local businesses is a powerful way to expand your sphere of influence, generate leads, and build strong community ties. By forming strategic partnerships, collaborating on events and promotions, and supporting each other's initiatives, you can create a network of trusted allies who can help you grow your real estate business. The key to success lies in building genuine, mutually beneficial relationships that contribute to both your business and the local community.

Action Steps

Identify Potential Business Partners:

- Research local businesses that align with your brand values and target market, such as home improvement stores, mortgage brokers, interior designers, or moving companies.
- Focus on businesses with strong community ties and a similar client base.

Initiate Contact and Build Relationships:

- Reach out to potential partners through personal introductions, offering value first, such as referring clients or offering real estate insights.
- Foster strong relationships through consistent communication and mutual support, ensuring reliability and trust-building over time.

Collaborate on Joint Initiatives:

- **Co-Host Events:** Plan joint events like homebuyer seminars, community fairs, or charity events to strengthen relationships and engage with potential clients.
- **Cross-Promotions:** Offer joint promotions, such as discounts or gift baskets, and promote each other's services through social media or newsletters.
- **Referral Networks:** Establish formal or informal referral agreements to send clients between businesses. Offer incentives or rewards for successful referrals.

Support Local Business Initiatives:

- Sponsor or participate in local events, such as community festivals or charity fundraisers, to build visibility and demonstrate your commitment to the community.
- Join local business associations or chambers of commerce to network with other professionals and foster collaboration opportunities.

Leverage Social Media:

- Highlight collaborations and cross-promotions with local businesses on your social media platforms. Share content that features local businesses and tag them to enhance visibility for both parties.

Track and Measure Success:

- Keep track of the referrals, leads, and business growth generated through local business partnerships.
- Evaluate the success of your collaborations and adjust your strategies to ensure your relationships are mutually beneficial and continue to provide value.

15

Deepening Relationships with Local Businesses

Building strong relationships with local businesses is just the beginning. Real estate professionals must focus on deepening these relationships over time to maximize the benefits of these partnerships. Long-term collaborations can lead to consistent referrals, co-branded marketing opportunities, and a stronger presence in the community. This chapter will explore advanced strategies for nurturing and expanding your relationships with local businesses, ensuring these partnerships remain fruitful and mutually beneficial for years.

The Importance of Long-Term Business Relationships

Long-term relationships with local businesses offer numerous advantages, including:

1. **Sustained Referrals**: A well-maintained relationship with a local business can lead to steady referrals. As the trust between you and the business grows, they will likely recommend your services to their customers regularly.

2. **Collaborative Growth**: By working closely with local businesses over time, you can collaborate on larger, more impactful projects that benefit both parties, such as community events or joint marketing campaigns.

3. **Community Leadership**: Being consistently involved with local businesses positions you as a leader in the community. This enhances your reputation and increases your influence within your sphere of influence.

4. **Loyalty and Trust**: These relationships can evolve over time into strong bonds based on mutual trust and loyalty. This trust can make your business more resilient during market fluctuations.

5. **Exclusive Opportunities**: As your relationships deepen, you may gain access to exclusive opportunities, such as first rights to co-sponsor events or priority referrals.

Advanced Strategies for Deepening Relationships

To take your business relationships to the next level, consider the following advanced strategies:

1. Create Exclusive Partnerships

Exclusive partnerships involve forming deeper, more committed collaborations with select local businesses. These partnerships are characterized by high trust and mutual investment, often resulting in unique opportunities not available to other real estate agents.

- **Exclusive Referrals**: Establish an agreement where local businesses refer all their clients exclusively to you for real estate needs. In return, you can offer exclusive benefits, such as priority referrals or special discounts for their clients.

- **Co-Branded Marketing Materials**: Develop co-branded marketing materials, such as flyers, brochures, or social media posts, that feature your real estate services and the local business. This type of collaboration helps both businesses reach a wider audience while strengthening the partnership.

- **Joint Ventures**: Consider launching joint ventures with local businesses, such as a community outreach program, a local podcast, or a shared office space. These ventures can provide significant visibility and reinforce the partnership.

2. Regular Check-Ins and Updates

Maintaining strong relationships requires regular communication. Stay in touch with your business partners through scheduled check-ins and updates to ensure your partnership remains strong.

- **Quarterly Meetings**: Schedule quarterly meetings with your business partners to discuss the progress of your collaboration, share updates, and plan future initiatives. These meetings can help address any challenges and keep the partnership on track.
- **Customized Reports**: Provide your business partners with customized reports highlighting your collaboration's results, such as the number of referrals received or the success of joint marketing campaigns. This transparency helps build trust and demonstrates the value of the partnership.
- **Personalized Touches**: Remember important dates, such as the anniversary of your partnership or the business owner's birthday. Sending a personalized note or small gift on these occasions can strengthen your bond and show that you value the relationship.

3. Offer Value-Added Services

One of the best ways to deepen a business relationship is to offer additional value beyond the initial agreement. Going the extra mile can create a stronger connection and demonstrate your commitment to the partnership.

- **Educational Workshops**: Offer to host educational workshops or seminars for the employees or customers of the local business. For example, you could provide a workshop on homebuying tips or real estate market trends, offering valuable insights that benefit their audience.

- **Employee Benefits Programs**: Develop an employee benefits program in collaboration with local businesses, offering special real estate services or discounts to their employees. This strengthens the relationship and expands your potential client base.

- **Customized Marketing Campaigns**: Create customized marketing campaigns that align with the local business's goals. For example, if the business is launching a new product or service, you could help promote it through your real estate marketing channels.

4. Engage in Community Initiatives Together

Engaging in community initiatives is a powerful way to deepen your relationship with local businesses while giving back to the community. Collaborative community involvement can lead to greater visibility and a stronger shared commitment to local causes.

- **Charity Fundraisers**: Partner with local businesses to organize charity fundraisers that benefit a cause you both care about. This could involve hosting a charity auction, sponsoring a local sports team, or organizing a charity walk.

- **Volunteer Together**: Volunteer together at local events or organizations, such as food drives, Habitat for Humanity projects, or community clean-up days.

Shared volunteer experiences can strengthen your bond and demonstrate your commitment to the community.

- **Community Sponsorships**: Co-sponsor community events, such as festivals, parades, or school events, with your business partner. This collaboration enhances your visibility and reinforces your shared commitment to the local area.

5. Leverage Technology for Collaboration

Technology can significantly deepen business relationships by facilitating communication, collaboration, and shared marketing efforts.

- **Shared CRM Systems**: Use a shared customer relationship management (CRM) system to manage referrals, track leads, and monitor the success of joint initiatives. This transparency helps ensure both parties are aligned and can easily access important information.
- **Co-Hosted Webinars**: Collaborate on co-hosted webinars that provide valuable information to both of your audiences. Webinars effectively reach a wider audience and position both businesses as experts in your respective fields.
- **Joint Social Media Campaigns**: Leverage social media platforms to run joint campaigns, such as giveaways, contests, or promotions. Use hashtags, tags, and cross-posting to maximize reach and engagement.

Case Studies: Deepening Relationships with Local Businesses

To illustrate the impact of deepening relationships with local businesses, let's examine a few case studies:

Case Study 1: Long-Term Partnership with a Moving Company

A real estate agent established a long-term partnership with a local moving company, starting with a simple referral agreement. Over time, the partnership evolved into an exclusive arrangement where the moving company referred all their clients to the agent. In return, the agent offered moving discounts to their clients and included the moving company in all open house events. This partnership resulted in a steady stream of referrals, increased visibility for both businesses, and a strong bond based on mutual trust.

Case Study 2: Co-Branding with a Local Coffee Shop

A realtor partnered with a popular local coffee shop to create a series of co-branded marketing materials, including flyers, social media posts, and a co-hosted event. The partnership began with simple cross-promotions but grew into a deeper collaboration that included co-sponsored community events and exclusive discounts for the coffee shop's customers. The co-branded materials helped both businesses reach new audiences and reinforced their presence in the community.

Case Study 3: Joint Community Initiatives with a Home Improvement Store

A real estate agent and a local home improvement store teamed up to sponsor several community initiatives, including a charity home renovation project and a community garden. These initiatives benefited the local community and strengthened the partnership between the agent and the store. The collaboration led to increased referrals, enhanced credibility in the community, and a shared commitment to local causes.

Action Item: Deepening Relationships with Local Businesses

To deepen your relationships with local businesses, follow these steps:

Step 1: Evaluate Existing Partnerships

Review your current business relationships and identify opportunities for deeper collaboration. Consider which partnerships have the potential for long-term growth and mutual benefit.

Step 2: Initiate Advanced Strategies

Implement advanced strategies such as exclusive partnerships, value-added services, and joint community initiatives to strengthen your business relationships.

Step 3: Maintain Regular Communication

Schedule regular check-ins and updates with your business partners to ensure your relationships remain strong and aligned with your mutual goals.

Deepening relationships with local businesses is crucial in expanding your sphere of influence and achieving long-term success in the real estate industry. By focusing on advanced strategies, such as exclusive partnerships, regular communication, value-added services, and community engagement, you can build stronger, more resilient relationships that benefit both your business and the local community. These deepened relationships will lead to more referrals and collaborative opportunities and establish you as a trusted and integral member of your local business network.

Action Steps

Evaluate Existing Partnerships:

- Review your current relationships with local businesses and assess which ones have the potential for deeper collaboration.
- Consider the quality and longevity of your partnerships, and look for opportunities to grow them.

Initiate Advanced Strategies:

- **Exclusive Partnerships:** Offer exclusive referrals, co-branded marketing materials, or joint ventures with trusted partners.
- **Value-Added Services:** Provide additional value, such as educational workshops, employee benefits programs, or customized marketing campaigns.
- **Community Initiatives:** Co-host charity fundraisers, volunteer together, or sponsor community events to increase visibility and show commitment to local causes.

Maintain Regular Communication:

- Schedule quarterly meetings or regular check-ins with your business partners to keep relationships strong and aligned with shared goals.
- Share updates and track the success of your collaborative efforts, fostering transparency and trust.

Leverage Technology:

- Use shared CRM systems to monitor referrals and track lead progress.
- Co-host webinars, run joint social media campaigns, and use online tools to collaborate more effectively and reach a wider audience.

Develop Co-Branding Opportunities:

- Create co-branded marketing materials, such as flyers or social media posts, and promote each other's services to strengthen both businesses' presence in the community.
- Celebrate Successes Together:
- Acknowledge milestones and successes in your partnership, such as anniversaries or successful campaigns, and publicly celebrate them to reinforce the relationship.

Conclusion
Unleashing Your Potential to Nurture Your Sphere of Influence

Nurturing your sphere of influence is not just a strategy; it's an art that combines relationship-building, effective communication, and community engagement. Throughout this book, we've explored several ways to cultivate and expand your sphere, each designed to empower you as a real estate professional to build stronger connections, earn more referrals, and, ultimately, grow your business. Now, as we bring all these concepts together, it's time to reflect on how these strategies interconnect and how you can confidently apply them to create a thriving real estate practice.

The Power of Relationships

A network of strong, trusted relationships is at the heart of every successful real estate business. From leveraging your existing connections to forming new ones, nurturing your sphere of influence begins and ends with people. Each chapter in this book has provided you with tools to deepen these relationships, whether through personalized touches, regular communication, or meaningful engagements.

The most important takeaway here is that relationships are not transactional; they are built on trust, mutual respect, and a genuine interest in the well-being of others. As you apply the strategies from this book, always remember that the foundation of your success lies in the quality of the relationships you cultivate.

Consider the various ways you can connect with your sphere: personal outreach, providing valuable content, and hosting events are just a few examples. Each of these actions demonstrates your commitment to your clients and your community. By focusing on building authentic relationships, you will not only nurture your sphere of influence but also create a network of advocates who will support your business for years to come.

The Role of Consistency

Consistency is another crucial element in nurturing your sphere. As you've learned, a one-time effort is not enough to maintain a thriving network. The consistent, ongoing engagement keeps you top of mind with your clients and connections.

Throughout the book, we discussed various methods to stay connected, from regular check-ins and follow-ups to maintaining an active presence on social media. Each strategy reinforces your brand and keeps your name at the forefront of your sphere's thoughts. The key is to make consistency a habit, integrating these practices into your daily or weekly routine.

Consider setting up a schedule for your outreach efforts. For instance, you might dedicate certain days of the week to making phone calls, sending out newsletters, or updating your social media channels. By establishing a routine, you ensure you're consistently engaging with your sphere, which keeps your relationships strong and your business thriving.

The Importance of Value-Driven Interactions

In every interaction, whether with a potential client, a referral partner, or a local business, the value you provide will determine the strength of the relationship. People remember those who have genuinely helped them, who have offered solutions to their problems, and who have made a positive impact on their lives.

This book has provided numerous examples of how you can offer value to your sphere, from sharing market insights to providing referrals for other services. The goal is to position yourself not just as a real estate agent but as a trusted advisor and a valuable resource.

When you approach your interactions with a mindset of giving rather than receiving, you build trust and loyalty. Your sphere will see you as someone who genuinely cares about their needs, which naturally leads to more referrals and repeat business. Always ask yourself how you can add value in every situation, and your efforts will be rewarded.

The Power of Personalization

One of the recurring themes in this book is the importance of personalization. A personal touch can make all the difference in a world where people are bombarded with generic messages and automated emails. Whether it's a handwritten note, a custom-tailored marketing piece, or a face-to-face meeting, personalized interactions show your clients and connections that they matter.

We've explored various ways to personalize your approach, from segmenting your email list to creating custom content for different segments of your sphere. The more you can tailor your interactions to your client's specific needs and interests, the more effective your efforts will be.

Remember that personalization is not just about addressing someone by their first name; it's about understanding their unique situation and providing relevant solutions. As you implement the strategies from this book, always consider how you can make each interaction more personal and meaningful.

Engaging with the Community

Another critical aspect of nurturing your sphere of influence is your engagement with the community. By actively participating in local events, supporting local businesses, and contributing to community initiatives, you strengthen your relationships and enhance your reputation as a real estate professional who cares about the community.

Throughout this book, we've discussed various ways to get involved, from sponsoring local events to collaborating with local businesses. These efforts help you build a stronger network and position you as a leader in the community. People are more likely to work with and refer business to someone actively contributing to the community's well-being.

Your involvement in the community also provides you with opportunities to connect with people who may not yet be in your sphere. Being visible and active increases your chances of meeting new clients and expanding your network.

Leveraging Technology

In today's digital age, technology plays a significant role in nurturing your sphere of influence. Technology offers numerous tools to enhance your efforts, from CRM systems that help you manage your contacts and communications to social media platforms that allow you to stay connected with your audience.

Throughout this book, we've covered various ways to leverage technology, including email marketing, social media, and online advertising. These tools can help you reach a larger audience, stay organized, and track the success of your efforts.

However, it's important to remember that technology should complement, not replace, the personal touch. Use these tools to enhance your relationships, not to automate them. The most successful real estate professionals are those who blend technology with personal interaction, creating a seamless and effective approach to nurturing their sphere.

Action Steps for Success

As you conclude this book, it's important to take actionable steps to implement what you've learned. Here's a simple plan to get started:

1. **Review Your Sphere**: Begin by reviewing your current sphere of influence. Identify key relationships

that need nurturing and areas where you can expand your network.

2. **Set Goals**: Establish clear, measurable goals for your nurturing efforts. Whether it's increasing the number of referrals you receive, enhancing your social media presence, or deepening your relationships with local businesses, having specific goals will help guide your efforts.

3. **Create a Schedule**: Develop a consistent schedule for your outreach efforts. This could include daily, weekly, or monthly tasks, such as making phone calls, sending emails, or hosting events.

4. **Personalize Your Approach**: Identify ways to personalize your interactions with your sphere. This could involve segmenting your email list, creating custom marketing materials, or offering tailored solutions to your clients' needs.

5. **Engage with the Community**: Look for opportunities to get involved in your local community. Attend events, sponsor local initiatives, and collaborate with local businesses to build your presence and strengthen your relationships.

6. **Leverage Technology**: Use technology to enhance your efforts. Invest in a CRM system to manage your contacts, use social media to stay connected with your audience, and track the success of your campaigns.

7. **Measure Your Success**: Regularly review your progress and adjust your strategies as needed. Use metrics such as referral rates, engagement levels, and client feedback to measure your success and refine your approach.

Encouragement for the Journey Ahead

As you embark on the journey of nurturing your sphere of influence, remember that success doesn't happen overnight. It's a process that requires time, effort, and dedication. However, with the right strategies in place, you can build a powerful network that will support your business for years to come.

Believe in your ability to make a difference in the lives of your clients and connections. Every interaction you have is an opportunity to build trust, offer value, and strengthen your relationships. By consistently applying the strategies in this book, you will create a thriving sphere of influence that not only benefits your business but also enhances your reputation as a trusted real estate professional.

Remember, the key to success is taking action. Start small, be consistent, and stay focused on your goals. Over time, you'll see the results of your efforts in the form of stronger relationships, more referrals, and a growing business.

In closing, I want to encourage you to take what you've learned and put it into practice. The tools and strategies in this book are designed to empower you to succeed. You have everything you need to nurture your sphere of influence and build a thriving real estate business. So go out there, take action, and watch your business grow. The journey ahead is full of opportunities, and with the right approach, you can achieve great success.

To your success!

Cheers,

About the Author

Hi there! I'm a real estate broker who's been passionate about "Impacting Lives Through Real Estate" since I first got licensed in 2013. And when I say passionate, I mean it. I sold my very first property for $12,500 (yes, you read that correctly). Let's just say the commission from that sale wouldn't exactly buy me a year's supply of cold brew coffee… but it did buy me invaluable experience and a great story to share!

Fast forward to today: I'm proud to own and operate Coldwell Banker Crown Realtors. In 2020, we took the leap to purchase the company, and it's been an incredible journey ever since. We've grown from one location to seven, increased our gross commission income from under $1 million to over $5.3 million, and even landed a spot on the Inc. 5000 2024 Fastest Growing Companies list. It's been a whirlwind, but I wouldn't trade it for anything (except maybe a new Apple gadget. I'm a total sucker for iPhones, iPads, iAnything).

Beyond running the brokerage, I'm a graduate of the Anywhere Real Estate Ascend Program and hold several professional designations from the National Association of REALTORS®. But fancy letters after my name mean nothing without a true commitment to helping people. My mission is to serve clients through a personalized and technology-forward approach, like using the latest real estate tools so you can sign documents on your phone while sipping your own cold brew in your pajamas. (I won't judge.)

When I'm not working on deals or brainstorming the next office expansion, you can usually find me enjoying life in Alexandria, MN, with family. We love spending time on the lake, especially kicking back on a pontoon, where the only pressing question is whether we have enough snacks for the kids. (Spoiler alert: We never do.)

I'm also deeply involved in my community, partnering with Habitat for Humanity to support affordable housing initiatives, and actively supporting our local Community Christian Schools. It's all part of my aim to create an impact both inside and outside the office. In addition, I've been fortunate enough to share my passion through speaking engagements, teaching real estate agents and sales professionals how to cultivate their sphere of influence in a meaningful (and hopefully entertaining) way.

If you're looking for a real estate experience that's as personalized as your Spotify playlist—and want to work with someone who values relationships over transactions—you're in the right place. Drop me a line, and let's see how we can make your real estate dreams a reality...preferably over a cold brew!